The 1984–1985 Miners' Strike in Nottinghamshire

Also available from Pen & Sword Books Ltd

The Miners' Strike Day by Day
The Illustrated Diary of Yorkshire Miner Arthur Wakefield

Brian Elliott (ed) ISBN 1 903425 16 6

Yorkshire's Flying Pickets in the 1984–85 Miners' Strike
Based on the Diary of Silverwood Miner Bruce Wilson

Brian Elliott (ed) ISBN 1 903425 51 4

The 1984-1985 Miners' Strike in Nottinghamshire

'If Spirit Alone Won Battles'

THE DIARY OF JOHN LOWE

MINING HERITAGE
SERIES

Edited by
Jonathan Symcox

Wharncliffe Books

First published in Great Britain in 2011
and reprinted in 2015 by
WHARNCLIFFE BOOKS
An imprint of
Pen & Sword Books Ltd
47 Church Street
Barnsley, South Yorkshire
S70 2AS

ISBN 978 1 84563 144 4

A CIP catalogue record for this book is available from the British Library

Typeset in 10/12pt Century
By Concept, Huddersfield, West Yorkshire

Printed and bound in England
By CPI Group (UK) Ltd, Croydon, CR0 4YY

Pen & Sword Books Ltd incorporates the Imprints of Aviation, Atlas,
Family History, Fiction, Maritime, Military, Discovery, Politics, History,
Archaeology, Select, Wharncliffe Local History, Wharncliffe True Crime,
Military Classics, Wharncliffe Transport, Leo Cooper, The Praetorian Press,
Remember When, Seaforth Publishing and Frontline Publishing.

For a complete list of Pen & Sword titles please contact
PEN & SWORD BOOKS LIMITED
47 Church Street, Barnsley, South Yorkshire, S70 2AS, England
E-mail: enquiries@pen-and-sword.co.uk
Website: www.pen-and-sword.co.uk

CONTENTS

FOREWORD

by Dennis Skinner MP

I knew John Lowe growing up and as a young man in Clay Cross. I passed him thousands of times in the street, going to work, coming back from work, going to a council meeting, going for the paper, doing this, doing that. But I cannot recall talking with him politically, except regarding the local elections. 'Have you been, John? Have you voted?' I'd ask. And he'd nod and say: 'Yes, you know I have.' But that was it.

We went our separate ways, as happens. He went to live in Nottinghamshire to work and I thought no more about it. Then years later, in 1984, the national miners' strike began and I came across him again. He may well have been active in the miners' victorious strikes of the 1970s, but they were very short, six or seven weeks. This one was to be different. Early in the dispute I did a big meeting at Worksop set up principally to try and galvanise the local NUM forces in Nottinghamshire. And there was John Lowe – and he wasn't just a member of the crowd! He was asking questions, making speeches ... I had to say to someone: is that the same fella? And the reply was *yes*!

It was a revelation to me because for the rest of the strike and way beyond John Lowe was one of six or a dozen key figures in Nottinghamshire. He was there at everything. After the strike he would organise the Black and Gold at places like Rainworth and Blidworth and all over. If I was to be asked whether people could turn into giants, politically and industrially, as a result of a battle with the management and the Government and the police ... I would put him in my top ten of those people. I rate him exceptionally highly. Most people who got involved in the leadership of the strike you could have named before the event. Ida Hackett – we all knew she'd be kicking the ball about. Sid Richmond – he was waiting for it. It was made for him! And various others I could mention. But you would not have named John Lowe. Yet when it began, he was on the front row.

I cannot say with certainty that he was transformed by events: it may have been latent, there all the time, and he was just waiting for the day, for the year – and those that followed – to bring it out. There are surprising people in all walks of life that become strong when things are exceptionally difficult. I could give examples of people in the Bolsover area, but not as sharply distinctive as John Lowe, he that I knew as a miner in Clay Cross and who then became a leader for several years in the most difficult coalfield in Britain. He shone out among the others in terms of being a discovery.

Believe me, it was hard in Nottinghamshire. You had to be strong to survive: in many of those pits there were more people in work than there were on the picket line. Picketing there was for real: they were trying to stop their friends – erstwhile friends – and, I suppose, some enemies from going through the picket line day after day, after day. While the Government and everybody else regarded the scabs as decent, honest, genuine people who should be allowed a free route to get to work, this relatively small band of folk were doing the honourable, principled thing of being prepared to eat grass rather than give in. They are not given honours, OBEs and the like, for their gallantry; but if they were handed out to such people on that side of the political fence, John would have been a recipient, without a doubt. But he'd tell you he didn't believe in the system anyway.

Much of the Notts workforce came from other areas of the country. It was very significant during the strike that pits like Cotgrave, dominated by those from the North East, could not emulate what their colleagues were doing up there; and yet I remember opening a gala at Cotgrave long before the strike and they were running the whippets and everything else – it was like a little bit of Durham. But they acted like Notts miners, not Durham miners, at the end. Those leading the fight at National level always knew Notts might renege upon what the rest of us were doing, as they had in the old days in the General Strike of 1926, so we had to concentrate upon the county. I know that John believed that Spencerism was still prevalent: they were not only dealing with the present situation, but also the history. The Notts coalfield, generally speaking, made a lot of money: as it was newer than the others, at most pits you did not have to go so far out to fetch the coal as in the other areas. The colliers there used to get wages that were a little bit above the odds. All this meant that they thought they were the bee's knees – indispensable. And yet it wasn't about that. The working miners in Notts were promised the moon, and look at it now: I think there's one pit left. So what was it all for? John and others were trying to convey that message the best way they could; they certainly weren't telling lies and they were treated like shit, even when it was over. So even though Notts was one of the newest coalfields in Britain, with pits that had a longer life than almost anywhere else in Britain, it has now almost entirely disappeared. That's the price the scabs paid.

The county is now like any other struggling former mining area: that economic power from the pits and the big manufacturing base around Nottingham has disappeared. The erosion of the Labour vote, the fragmentation which has led to the election of tin-pot mayors and all sorts, could not have taken place had the strike not been lost. I'm sure of that, because victory has a special glow about it. It makes you feel good. And we'd still have the pits. My constituency had a few thousand that worked over the border in Notts while there were also several thousand on strike. I still see a lot of them when they have a problem, be it housing, social security or whatever. I deliberately raise the strike, even today, in order to see what their reaction is – and many of them prefer to not enter that specific part of the discussion, and move the subject on to something else. They would rather not reflect on what happened.

As John writes, we needed a second front to see us to victory. I knew that one of our great strengths would be if the Government had to deal with another industrial dispute alongside that of the miners: the unions could not lose as, even if they did not give the Government that extra headache, their employer would have given in. If I had been at the top of the TUC I'd have told them to ask for everything – wages and conditions of all kinds. But the only ones we could get out were the dockers, for a short period. Part of my speechmaking all around the country was arguing that case right throughout the whole piece. You had to convey the idea that it was possible for the 13 million trade unionists to actually get involved in support of the miners, rather than just sending money, which to be fair to them they did. We had some difficulty with the power workers because of their right-wing leadership, but that wasn't true of other unions: a lot of them had left-wing leadership but didn't come out in support and that was a big disappointment to me. And when the mining deputies had their ballot and voted overwhelmingly to strike, they were bought off with the promise of a review of the pits. They were told by Thatcher and MacGregor: 'Don't worry. You'd don't have to go on strike. We can assure you that every single pit will go into a review and won't just close automatically.' And they bought it. Not one single pit that went into a review came out with a future. Not one.

John privately feared the worst, but one of the conditions for being a socialist is that you're an optimist. That's why I did something like 300 meetings in that year, and why John kept up his part throughout. I don't suppose for a minute that he was telling people quietly: 'We've had it, kid.' You didn't do that. You always believed that there was a glimmer of hope: that someone else might join the strike, that we might just beat them.

I look back at that time now with a mixture of agony and ecstasy. At all those meetings held here, there and everywhere to raise money for the miners I had to give a speech that made them laugh; I had to make them cry; I had to make them *think*; I had to send them home happy ... and I had to do it without telling lies. That was the agony. The support I saw around the country, even in the face of defeat and at the mercy of the press, was the

Dennis Skinner speaking at Durham miners' rally *(News Line)*

ecstasy. The agony of the T&G failing to get the dockers out on the east coast, where the imported coal was coming in, followed the ecstasy of July, when I opened at the Durham miners' rally with the words: 'The miners are out ... the sun's out ... and now the dockers are out!' Agony when the deputies were bought off after the ecstasy of August, when 70 per cent of them voted to strike. And the support from the Indian shopkeepers, the gays and lesbians, groups who knew what it was like to be attacked the way the miners were being attacked, was another ecstasy for me.

I remember speaking in Wimbledon for People Against Pit Closures and there was a lass from Creswell, in my constituency, and she was nearly crying. 'They want me to speak, Dennis,' she told me. I asked her: 'What have you been up to?' She said: 'We've had a lot of trouble: someone set fire to the soup kitchen.' I said: 'I know. UDM.' She said: 'That's what people are saying.' And I said: 'That's what I've heard, too. That's your speech. You tell them about your conditions and the UDM setting fire to your kitchen.' Normally they'd have the collection after I finished speaking – but when she got up they were all crying! She'd never made a speech before in her life, yet the fire was blazing; they were trying to put it out; these bastards were even stopping them from feeding people who haven't got anything to eat. That's the agony, and the ecstasy. So I said to the chair: 'Collection.' He said: 'No, we do it after you, Dennis.' And I said: 'Do it now, while they're all crying!'

Today we have 'generations of instant gratification' – they want it all and they want it now. They've got the credit cards, the mobile phones and all the rest, they've never had to struggle; kids have all the toys they need so they are brought up to believe they can have everything. The conditions are no longer there to form the strength of character and principle that could be seen in the likes of John Lowe during the strike. I'm not saying they cannot emerge; but they won't be as thick on the ground. John was made for the job: that he did not throw in the towel once the fight was lost shows that this tower of strength was the real John Lowe. It was there forever, ingrained in him right up to his death.

Cometh the hour, cometh the man.

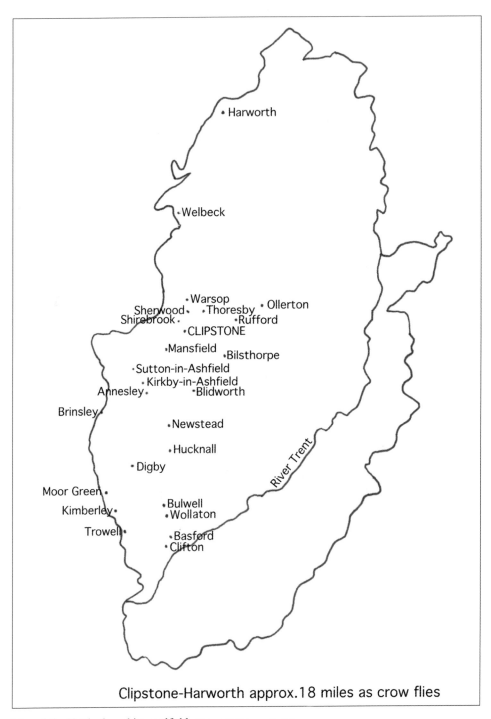

• Harworth

•Welbeck

•Warsop
Sherwood• •Thoresby • Ollerton
Shirebrook• •Rufford
•CLIPSTONE
•Mansfield
•Bilsthorpe
•Sutton-in-Ashfield
• Kirkby-in-Ashfield
Annesley• •Blidworth

Brinsley

•Newstead

•Hucknall

• Digby

Moor Green •
Kimberley•
Trowell•
•Bulwell
•Wollaton
•Basford
• Clifton

River Trent

Clipstone-Harworth approx.18 miles as crow flies

Map of the Nottinghamshire coalfield. *(Copyright Rebecca Tonks)*

INTRODUCTION AND ACKNOWLEDGEMENTS

by Jonathan Symcox

Back in the Eighties Grandad always seemed a larger-than-life figure to us kids, possessed a growling, good-humoured voice and was never short of an opinion. Visits to and parties at his and Grandma's house were always chaotic and fun-filled. Prominent in the house was something not understood until much later in life: amongst the family photographs and ornaments, lining the hallway and stairs, were commemorative plates and framed photographs speaking of the NUM; of the miners united remaining undefeated; of the 1984/85 strike. As years passed their significance gradually filtered through – and it became clear that this solitary year in Grandad's life meant everything to him.

He was a proud man, a family man, and given some of the painful events of that year, may have reflected with a degree of regret at how some things turned out. Yet no one can doubt that he was foremost a man of principle and honour: it shone through his commitment to colleagues at the pit, to his union, the industry he worked within from the age of fourteen and, of course, his class. Ask any friend who knew him and they will recall his gentle nature and unwavering dedication.

Grandad recorded his experience of the great pit strike for jobs in painstaking detail, a duty which often saw him up to the small hours, even when a 4am – or earlier – alarm clock awaited. Despite her unswerving loyalty, it drove Grandma crazy: he was in poor personal health owing to decades spent underground and was nearing retirement, while the stresses placed upon him by the dispute were huge. He strove for a clinical, fact-driven delivery but, out of necessity, also used the diary as a vent for the frustration he felt and for the anger generated deep within him. As such his record reads as of one constantly struggling against a tide of emotion to, as perfectly as possible, highlight the abuses to which the miners were subjected. What is contained within these pages is a mere snapshot of what he wrote at the time and afterwards: as editor I sought to convey as accurately as possible how he felt and acted day by day, with no attempt made to gloss over the grievances, petty or otherwise, which inevitably arise in such times of difficulty; nor have I toned down the sentiments and, on occasion, language that characterise his fury with those passing through the picket to work. But alongside the despair there is a deep well of hope for him to draw upon and one also of love and laughter.

In these times of job losses, pension cuts and protest, the 1984/85 strike resonates with the little man or woman as potently as ever before. John Lowe's diary is a priceless record of the most important of all industrial disputes, one that shaped the country we know today, from the very heart of the Notts battleground upon which the miners were ultimately impaled. But it is also the tale of a man, flesh and blood, who stood up for what he believed in; I hope that the reader will see this man, lost to us these last few years, within the pages and recognise a true working-class hero.

ACKNOWLEDGEMENTS

Many thanks are due to the following people:

All the family, for their love and support; Elsie Lowe, for her memories; and Andrew Symcox, for setting me on the way.

The ex-Notts NUM and Retired Miners' Association: Doug Broadfoot, Eric Eaton and Arthur Jackson.

Pendle Support Group: Tim Ormerod and Susan Nike.

Editor Jonathan Symcox contemplates Clipstone headstocks today *(Jonathan Symcox)*

News Line and Class War: Peter Arkell and Dave Douglass.

Pen and Sword/Wharncliffe Books: Brian Elliott.

Labour MPs: Vernon Coaker (Gedling), Jim Hood (Lanark & Hamilton East), Alan Meale (Mansfield), Gloria De Piero (Ashfield) and Dennis Skinner (Bolsover).

**News Line images are by Peter Arkell, Roy Rising,
Sean Smith and Katalin Arkell**

TRIBUTES TO JOHN LOWE

Alan Meale MP

Anyone who has ever experienced industrial conflict at first hand, its financial hardships, broken relationships and euphoria, will immediately understand the heartfelt meaning contained within the statement: 'A working-class hero is something to be.' It was out of such experiences that I found myself friends with John Lowe, a man who epitomised the unequal battle lines drawn before the members of the National Union of Mineworkers in Nottinghamshire. Unlike in other Areas, NUM membership in the county numbered in the mid-hundreds against the strike-breaking 14,000 of the Union of Democratic Mineworkers; but that never mattered to John. If anything, it made him more determined to succeed. It was because of such individual strength that the Union membership in work, redundant, sacked and retired was able to continue to meet and help one another, as shown in the formation and maintenance of the Black and Gold organisation, which John was at the heart of for its twenty years of existence. His organisational skills, quiet diplomacy and robust loyalty to his workmates and class will never be forgotten.

Norman Richmond

In my dad's early days down the mine the unions were just coming into being and such people as him were able to change things to make life a little bit easier for miners – and the generations following benefited from the stance they took. John Lowe and Sid Richmond came from a stronger generation: they had to be tough because life was hard. They were such characters, formed through their strong principles – and such people, for me, never die. They carry on through their families and through their stories – which serve as an example to us all.

Doug Broadfoot

Before the strike, anybody who lived in the pit village you knew – but you maybe didn't know them to talk to. John and Jim Dowen took charge of the Clipstone strikers and everyone out with them developed a good rapport and got to know each other really well. John's door was always open, at any time of the day, for us to discuss our problems or just go in for a natter. The name we gave him was General John: he and Jim were the generals, there was no getting away from it, and especially John as he was involved with the troops whereas Jim was higher up with the organisation. Everyone was happy with that arrangement – and John always led from the front. It was a sad day at his funeral – I know his close family were in a bit of a mess and that he meant a lot to many people.

Tim Ormerod
The Labour Party in Pendle readily agreed to adopt the Clipstone miners' women's support group early on in the coal industry's dispute. I was secretary of the Party at the time. One of the towns in Pendle, Nelson, was often called 'little Moscow' on account of its reputation during the textile strikes between the great wars. Support organisations were always quickly set up during that period and this attitude carried on over the years to recognise the struggle of the miners who were on strike. I travelled to Clipstone to spend time with the striking miners in that village and got to know John Lowe well; I am very pleased that his diaries have been published.

Elsie Lowe
We went to the local 'hop' together when we first met: Johnny was smart-looking, with immaculate hair, and walked tall – and that's how he was all his life. He promised to come to Matlock with me and my family and I didn't think he'd turn up, but he did; we both knew we'd be married after that. Family always came first with him: he was a great husband, father and grandfather. For him, black was black and white was white and he always followed that route. He always held his head up, no matter what. There's so much more I could say about him, but never do it justice.

A 'THOUGHT' FOR NOTTINGHAMSHIRE MINERS

Author unknown

First they came for the Welsh pits
And I did not speak out
Because I was not Welsh

Then they came for the Scottish pits
And I did not speak out
Because I was not Scottish

Then they came for the Yorkshire pits
And I did not speak out
Because I did not come from Yorkshire

Then they came for me
And there was no one left
To speak out for me

A SUMMARY OF MY LIFE

Born in Whiston in 1931, my early years were spent in that village on the outskirts of Rotherham in South Yorkshire. During my school years, which included the 1939–45 period of the Second World War, I lived with my mother and stepfather in the North Derbyshire pit village of Danesmoor, approximately five miles from Chesterfield. I left school at fourteen years of age in 1945. After working for a brief period at the Clay Cross Companies coking plant, I left to begin work at Parkhouse Colliery, the local mine which was known locally as 'Catty' pit. Mining then became the only job I knew. In 1953 I married Elsie, a relationship that produced two sons and three daughters. They in turn have given us ten grandchildren. By the early 1960s I had left Parkhouse and moved to Rufford Colliery in North Nottinghamshire.

Several years later I moved over to Clipstone Colliery where, after forty years of employment underground, over thirty of which were at the coalface, I was finally made redundant in February 1987. Unfortunately, by that time a series of accidents were beginning to take their toll. Arthritic conditions of back and neck now have a severely limiting effect and physical activities or leisure pursuits requiring effort are very much restricted. Until the great 1984–85 dispute I was never a political activist, but was always a supporter of my union; both Elsie and myself took pleasure in a very close involvement for many years with the local Scout group. This took us into such things as fundraising, sporting activities and the general organisation of what was a very active group of people. That has now ended.

John Lowe on the picket line *(News Line)*

John Lowe
Clipstone 1991

PART ONE

APRIL–MAY 1984

This is one man's effort to record day by day the events at a North Nottinghamshire colliery where, to our <u>shame</u>, we waited for five weeks before joining the efforts of 80 per cent of the British coalfields in their opposition to 'Butcher MacGregor'.

All stories need a beginning, and in this particular one I was absent from work and attending the physiotherapy department of the Mansfield General hospital for the treatment of injuries sustained over the years which had become a persistent worry. The dispute had erupted around us and all I could do was to listen to the noises from the pit from a distance: night after night the noisy and angry confrontation was taking place as I lay uncomfortably in bed. Unfortunately for the cause, the Yorkshire lads had come down prepared to bully any opposition into submission. This policy not only proved counterproductive at the time but was to cause us problems in plenty in the long term.

Clipstone village layout *(Copyright Rebecca Tonks)*

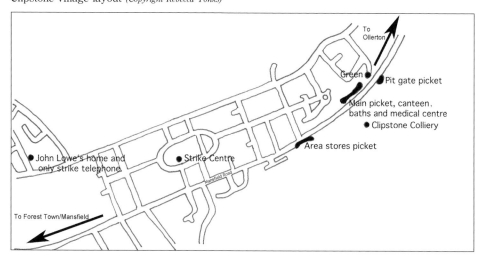

I was signed off sick after the dispute had been in progress for three weeks. The following fortnight caused me much soul searching and mental conflict. I was certainly aware that a strike was in progress and the hard part was the realisation that I was not part of it. Things were now quiet at the Clipstone Colliery with no sign of picketing taking place. What I did not know was that the police were keeping any potential pickets well away from the pit so I was never actually crossing a picket line on my way to work. Without either Local or Area leadership involvement, a great many of the membership were not prepared to show any commitment and at that stage, knowing as little as I did, I cannot say I blamed them. With nothing happening at our pit, my mental torture continued for the next two weeks and with the monthly branch meeting due, I realised that for the first time I now had an opportunity to do something positive. I made contact with my brother-in-law, Dennis Musson, who worked at the Markham Colliery in North Derbyshire. After a lengthy telephone conversation, he agreed to contact some of his colleagues and to lobby our meeting the next morning. Up to this point I had not spoken to anyone at Clipstone about action of any kind. Although I had decided that I had to become personally involved in some way, I still had no thoughts as to how it would be achieved.

Anti-Notts feeling among Yorkshire's men and women *(News Line)*

On the Sunday morning of the meeting, April 15th 1984, the lads from Derbyshire duly arrived and took up a position outside the welfare hall. A few of us joined them in what I hoped would be a show of solidarity and, although there was some mild abuse, the majority of those entering avoided making any response at that stage. The hall was packed solid and was the best-attended meeting I have ever seen in my years in the industry, a golden opportunity for the branch leadership to show some courage. Almost immediately the discussion and argument was centred on the dispute. With the benefit of hindsight, I can see that events that morning were to shape the attitudes of those present. Unfortunately they decided to swim with the tide of the 'anti' feeling that was being noisily put across and I fear that many waverers looking for a lead decided to do likewise. Excuses, bitterness, half-truths and innuendos were all being fired by people whose professed socialist views and principles should have helped put them firmly on our side. How hollow their utterances have since proved to be; how cynical a reputation they have built for themselves.

The meeting deteriorated throughout and when warnings were given of the dangers of 'Spencerism'[1] and possible breakaways, the response from the 'antis' was a tumultuous cheer. Looking back, what I found most difficult to accept was that most of the noise opposing us came from people who had only been in the industry for a relatively short time and obviously felt no loyalty to their brothers in other NUM Areas. In a different economic climate, most would never have been found anywhere near a pit – butchers, bakers, candlestick makers. I felt sick at heart and powerless in the face of such mindless hate. Midway through the proceedings, I had taken as much as I could stomach and invited like-minded colleagues to stand outside.

Sunday 15 April

Monthly branch meeting at 9.30am and twelve Derbyshire lads were outside lobbying; approximately 600–700 men inside. Discussion centred around the dispute. At one point I stood and asked just how much we were prepared to take or if we were going to stand up and fight the closure programme. Here I was shouted down by the 'weekend' regulars. Such was the disgust that I felt, my final words were: 'If there are any men left here with red blood in their veins, they'll follow me outside now and stand beside those Derbyshire lads.' The invitation was accepted by around fifty men almost immediately.

Monday 16 April

Walking through the village to the pit this morning with my placards, my footsteps seemed to echo hollowly through the avenues. I feel alone and vulnerable in an alien world. Picket line established at 4.30am; gradual response but various excuses made, for example:

(a) Strike not official
(b) Want a national ballot
(c) Go with the majority

After the midday picket there was a meeting at the miners welfare, with around 100 present, where a strike committee was elected. With none of our elected branch officials with us, we had to accept the fact that we would be a 'rank and file' committee. Action and strategy was discussed in depth. Finance was considered of prime importance at this stage; the treasurers have undertaken a mammoth task.

Notes from initial Clipstone strike committee meeting *(John Lowe)*

Clipstone Colliery Strike Committee

Chairman.   John E Lowe .
Vice Chairman   Harry Haupham
Secretary   Len Marshall
Treasurer   Jim Dowen

Committee .   B Jeffries
                              C Fisher
                              J Strachan
                              K Davcen
                              C Nibbles
                              R Hartley

Notts ~~Area~~ ~~Strike~~ ~~Committee~~ x
Notts Rank & File Committee

Chairman   Mick Walker
Secretary   Paul Whetton

Treasurers   Jim Dowen   ½ Notts Miners Forum
                              Mick M'Ginty

Clipstones 2 Delegates   John E Lowe
                                    Phil Stout

22

Tuesday 17 April

Three-shift picket maintained; difficult to estimate results but the afternoon and night shifts seemed to be crippled. The media have been ignoring the Notts miners' efforts and misreporting as usual – we have complained to Yorkshire TV, Radio Nottingham and Radio Trent. Four cars were sent to Blidworth Colliery at their own expense; all got through police roadblocks. Decided to make committee men responsible for picket – two per shift. Jim Dowen our treasurer is travelling continually, talking to trades councils etc – the object is to raise money quickly.

Wednesday 18 April

Heavy picket being maintained on all three shifts; unconfirmed reports from inside the pit suggest that production is seriously disrupted, with attendance cut drastically and man-power really stretched. Five cars sent to Thoresby Colliery but only one reached there due to police roadblocks; some small donations received – Young Socialists, £6.50 – enough to give us a start with petrol money. Channel 4 cameras here this morning. Position still very fluid but managing to get the best of the situation through negotiation with police e.g. fifteen-man picket for Monday and Tuesday, cut to ten this afternoon. The response and discipline of the men has been magnificent. Meeting of the Area strike committee at 1.30pm at Ollerton: good progress reported from picket lines throughout the Area, while strategy was discussed in some detail.

Thursday 19 April

Progress halted today; now we grit our teeth and hang on to what we have. Heavy picket this morning but the afternoon shift is going to be thinned out.

Doug and Gus Broadfoot on Sheffield march *(Doug Broadfoot)*

Clipstone miners lobby NUM HQ *(News Line)*

The spirit of the men is such that when volunteers were asked for on the afternoon picket, instead of going to the demonstration and lobby in Sheffield, we did not fill the bus. The Sheffield contingent returned for the night shift full of emotion and enthusiasm. Supt. H of county police has been upsetting the arrangements with the officer in charge – our limits are to be renegotiated shift by shift. Sometimes we're cut back, then we regain lost ground; it depends on our success at negotiating. The police have been threatening to arrest anyone found distributing the leaflet entitled 'Portrait of a Scab' by Jack London[2] in 1929.

Friday 20 April

Morning turnout fair, but no progress. Mid-morning lobby at Berry Hill delegate conference: Richardson[3] and Chadburn[4] confirmed the strike was official from the announcement in Sheffield yesterday, but they didn't phone the Clipstone NUM office as we asked. This caused problems and confusion as our branch officials would not move before hearing from them.

Afternoon picket was well-attended with everything hanging on what happened at Area. Strike meeting held in the afternoon at the welfare; well-attended but more confusion when the delegate conference returned their usual waffling report. I had the feeling that this time we really had them. All that was needed was for Clipstone branch president Sid Walker to join us on the picket line; unfortunately it was not to be as he went home instead, unwilling to join us.

24

Henry Richardson announces that strike is official *(News Line)*

Evening picket well-attended: very few went through. Branch committee meeting tonight at 7.30pm to decide 'if they will join us'. Result of the meeting:

(a) Yes, we were official
(b) Yes, they would respect the picket line
(c) They would talk to the men on Tuesday morning and afternoon and tell them the position
(d) They would call a meeting for Tuesday night at the welfare to decide their own position
(e) The Union office would be kept open with minimum staff to cater for both working and striking miners

> The only member of our strike committee who had any experience of branch committee work was Jim Dowen, who had served as branch delegate for a number of years. He agreed to act as treasurer – at that time he was, in effect, a treasurer without funds, and had the responsibility of generating from somewhere the necessary finance that would enable us to proceed with the strike. I was asked to take on the chairmanship of the group, a task I readily agreed to do. Had I been possessed of a crystal ball, and been able to appreciate what acceptance would entail, my feelings might have been somewhat different.

The geography of the Clipstone pit is such as to make it a very difficult place to cover with a traditional picket. The whole complex straddles the Mansfield–Ollerton road. On the one side lies the pit top area and on the other stands the canteen, baths and medical centre. The two sides are connected by a tunnel under the road which is only accessible from the inside of the baths. Entrances there were in abundance and an effective picket needed to cover as many as we possibly could.

Besides maintaining a three-shift picket at the pit, the first week saw us sending out flying pickets to Thoresby and Blidworth Collieries; in addition we sent a large group to a demonstration and lobby of our national offices in Sheffield. Everyone was positive and full of enthusiasm. Jim Dowen and myself had attended three meetings at the Ollerton miners welfare that had seen the formation of an Area strike committee; here Jim became treasurer without resources once again, this time a joint appointment with Mick McGinty of the Ollerton Branch.

By the end of the first week we felt a grim sense of satisfaction with the way things were going. Although the problems facing us were mountainous, they did not at that stage seem insurmountable. I was convinced it was only a matter of time before everyone would join with us. By the second week the Yorkshire lads were getting through to us in large numbers, very often after a lot of hassle from the police: they would be turned back many times at roadblocks before getting near to any pit. As they became familiar with the area, their knowledge of minor roads and even cart tracks became invaluable to them. We had seen an invasion of our village by the police on an unbelievable scale: from dawn to dusk, two-man foot patrols were everywhere while Transit vans full of uniformed officers cruised throughout the day. The extensive use of roadblocks throughout Nottinghamshire not only saw them encircle the county to keep out the Yorkshire and Derbyshire strikers, but also restrict our movements within it – between pit and pit and pit and home. We were sewn up tight! The legality of this overkill – devised and operated by Charles McLachlan, Chief Constable of Nottinghamshire – was, we were repeatedly told, questionable to say the least. Later, when the screws were tightened further, light spotter planes and helicopters were used extensively, dogs and horses were available at very short notice and reinforcements were positioned at strategic points for instant deployment. Plain-clothed 'anti-intimidation' squads were sent into the villages ready to pounce on any allegation of violence or the threat of it. If it had not been so serious, the whole situation would have been downright laughable.

Sunday 22 April

Phone calls and contacts throughout the weekend. Need for strike committee to meet tomorrow to decide, if and when the branch committee join us, who takes responsibility for what.

Monday 23 April

Strike committee meeting at my house to discuss how we approach first shift back on Tuesday: decided to carry on to the first meeting once we have finished with the picket line and be ready to work with branch officials, if they join us.

Tuesday 24 April

Good turnout for the early picket; support from other pits was good with quite a few Yorkshiremen here – very noisy but orderly. Branch officials were, as we understood it, to talk to the men in the canteen and explain that we were an official picket line and as such should not be crossed. In actual fact branch secretary Alf Hemsley sat in the canteen and was not seen to address the men at all. Carrington, the branch delegate to the Area Council, came late and did talk to them – but also stated that anyone who wanted to work could work, thus encouraging strike-breaking. No wonder the men are confused. They were really disappointed as they were hoping for some commitment from the elected officials.

Noon picket saw one man arrested – he was from Ollerton. I was quite near when it happened and can quite honestly say that the lad was doing nothing different from the rest of the lads. Disgraceful! Night shift has been discontinued, with so many men off. This eases our job.

Full pit meeting at Clipstone welfare at 8.30pm. This resulted in the most disgraceful reaction that I have ever seen: speakers from both sides were numerous but when 'Spencerism' was mentioned as a danger, the result from the other side was one of cheers and shouts. When the break-up of the Union was brought up, this was openly encouraged again, to cheers. We made ourselves heard but with no commitment from any of our elected officials, the many, many waverers were not felt to be with us. I felt physically sick.

Ollerton striker arrested at Clipstone *(News Line)*

Wednesday 25 April

Still maintaining our grip with the early picket, and very few went through in the afternoon, but we need something to happen to boost the lads. Full branch officials' meeting at Berry Hill should hopefully bring something our way.

There they were told by National president Scargill that they should get in line and behind the men. He reiterated full endorsement for National Executive Council decision in Sheffield on Thursday last. Branch officials were later still looking for and putting different interpretations on that announcement. They have no intention of joining us and we can only assume they are looking to June and the branch elections. This is not responsible trade union leadership! Names of coal lorries being monitored. We estimate that only about a third of the men are at work and a whisper tells us that the management are considering three to four days of production and the rest maintenance and bye-work – this on two shifts.

Thursday 26 April

Some of our support has drifted back to work and more men are going through. Less men are joining the picket line, although many more remain not at work; about sixty to seventy pickets is the average number. Went with H Harpham to Berry Hill for whatever help was available – what a laugh. Chadburn promised to ask in Executive meeting this morning for buses for each branch for rally at Worksop on Saturday, and cash to finance picketing at each pit. Area Executive meeting result:

(a) £300 to each branch to be used for picketing only
(b) One bus per branch paid by Area for rally in Worksop
(c) All posters, badges and stick badges to be supplied by Area
(d) Instruct all branch officials to abide by National special conference decision not to cross picket lines and not to canvass against it

Lorry passes Clipstone picket line *(News Line)*

They are to give all facilities to men on strike. On receiving this information, I was convinced that there had to be some commitment at least from some of them. Sadly, NO – to their shame. Coal lorries still being monitored and contact with the T&G[5] again made. L[6] took lists of firms to them – they said they would contact us after a check. Chesterfield strike HQ called me: they have nothing for us but promise to let me know when they have. Shame again on our own Area! Some phone contact with strike HQ at Cortonwood – they need places for their men to stay in Notts to beat roadblocks. Situation this morning when the men asked to speak with delegate Carrington: I went to the Union office and asked – he said he'd be ten minutes but by 7pm, forty minutes later, he'd failed to show. Opinion was they didn't want to face the men. Actions speak louder than words.

Friday 27 April

Early picket – more men back at work. Not as many on picket line – around fifty to sixty. Back to pit at 10am to see Sid Walker; unfortunately there are many things we can still only do through the branch office:

(a) Bus booked for Saturday morning
(b) Use of the branch banner was refused; excuse was that a request has to go through branch
(c) Strike centre at Lido – Sid Walker countersigned application but told me M[7] says it is unavailable because repairs there are being carried out

Certain branch officials, notably Carrington, seem to be getting agitated; he is complaining that I put him on the spot yesterday by asking him to meet the men.

Finance is very low with more hardship cases coming in; Ollerton has 100. Money for petrol not now being paid. Tactics discussed at great length – some places having some success while most are struggling; a strategy was adopted to make one pit a permanent target until it fell. I'm not happy about leaving Clipstone with a token picket and losing what we have gained. One disgraceful incident today when a Yorkshire lad was arrested for parking his car: it was not illegally parked, was not causing a nuisance and was displaying a disabled disc. The man was obviously disabled and yet he was lifted by the police. The powers and authority that these people have adopted without challenge are awesome, sinister and very frightening. We learned today that C from Ollerton was arrested for the third time yesterday; he was kept in cells overnight and released this afternoon. He had had a rough time and had been taken to hospital with a suspected broken arm. His fifteen-year-old son was also handcuffed and taken with him.

At the Friday Area strike meeting a well-known local female activist Ida Hackett had been invited to talk of the role of the women's support group. This was a totally new perspective that had not at that time entered my mind. It had, however, been recognised elsewhere how important it was for this kind of support to get off the ground as soon as possible. We were told that the Nottinghamshire women's support group had pledged to help any local group get started. In common with the pit strike committees, however, who were also starting from scratch, any cash flow would have to be generated through their own efforts.

There was a difference that had to be recognised by all concerned: cash raised by the strikers was for the furtherance of the dispute and was not to be used to provide provisions for the various kitchens that sprang up. As for the women's groups, each one needed to organise its own support which would be backed up if need be by their own central committee. The success of this was to be proven a hundredfold in the months that followed.

We were beginning to realise at the Clipstone picket line how desperate our position was becoming. We were without a strike centre, had nowhere to hold our meetings and, even worse, we had no financial backing of any kind to provide the subsistence we were beginning to need – how we needed a support group of our own. Our hopes were realised on Saturday April 28th when a group of our women decided it was time they took a hand. Their first venture was a stall on the Mansfield marketplace, for which they needed a heart as big as a dustbin lid: they collected over £50 which, in the circumstances, was a magnificent achievement. Facing the public while seeking support for the strike in a place like this called for courage they proved capable of time and time again in the long term. The abuse they received only served to fire their determination. On the Sunday following, they held their first meeting and elected officers – Clipstone Women's Support Group was in business.

After two weeks on strike, we were beginning to realise the size of the problems that were facing us. We were standing picket against the sheer greed, fear and bloody mindedness of people in our midst – many of whom I would never have believed would cross a picket line. I had stood with many of these people in 1972 and 1974[8] in a display of solidarity that had won us a just settlement; now they were spurning our efforts to resist the clear threat to our very future. How safe they seemed to feel; how misguided they were.

Saturday 28 April
Bus for Worksop left on time with forty-five on board. Strike committee meeting held at my house.

Sunday 29 April
Another meeting of the strike committee: strategy for Monday decided, with the intention of toughening our attitude. Meeting at Sutton addressed by Arthur Scargill – solid attendance.

Monday 30 April
Media reporting that Yorkshire and North East miners packed the hall in Sutton yesterday; this is a gross misrepresentation of the facts, but he's still only preaching to the converted. The men were prepared to be lifted this morning – we asserted our rights and the police backed off.

Police toughened up this afternoon and the lads were given a pretty rough time. Pickets going to Thoresby for night shift; word is that Mansfield ladies' section will be there in some force.

G U I D E   T O   P I C K E T S

1. Picketing and Secondary Picketing <u>ARE NOT ILLEGAL</u> you cannot be arrested just for picketing.

2. The 1980 and 1982 Employment Act make certain forms of picketing 'unlawful' which means that your Union may be sued in the Court or an injunction sought to stop it.

3. You have a right to picket.

4. There is no law which limits the number of pickets to six. This is a guide issued by Tory Ministers and is not the law

5. <u>PICKETS CAN</u>

    *   talk to other workers to persuade them to strike
    *   talk to suppliers of goods and services to persuade them to stop carrying out their normal functions
    *   hand out leaflets explaining their cause
    *   move freely from one place to another

6. <u>CRIMINAL OFFENCES</u>

    *   using threatening behaviour
    *   using or threatening to use violence
    *   using intimidating words or behaviour
    *   obstructing the public highway
    *   carrying an offensive weapon
    *   causing criminal damage
    *   causing a breach of the peace
    *   acting in a manner which is reasonably likely to lead to a breach of the peace
    *   obstructing a police officer on duty

7. <u>PICKET ORGANISATION</u>

    *   there is <u>NO</u> obligation for there to be a Union Official on a picket. Your Union may prefer it but the police cannot insist on it.
    *   there is <u>NO</u> need to wear an 'Official Picket' badge.
    *   there is <u>NO</u> need to have an 'Official Picket' sign.

8. <u>IF ARRESTED OR STOPPED BY THE POLICE</u>

    *   say <u>NOTHING</u> that may be used against you
    *   show your NUM document on the back of this paper
    *   do not respond to Police violence
    *   call your NUM Office and request help
    *   fill in an incident report and obtain a witness

9. <u>REMEMBER</u>

    *   Picketing is your trade union right and is not illegal
    *   keep your cool and your head, don't be provoked
    *   report Police actions
    *   don't let the Police browbeat you, stand your ground and argue your rights to move freely and to picket

Sheet detailing pickets' legal rights *(John Lowe)*

MONDAY. 30·4-84.

ONLY 70 PICKETS TODAY.
THEY GOT A CHILLY RECEPTION
BUT HAD A WARM IN
THE CANTEEN AFTERWARDS.
THEY'VE STILL GOT PLENTY OF
CONCESSIONARY COAL AT
HOME, (THAT WE'RE SUPPLYING)

SO THEY SHOULD BE WARM
ENOUGH FOR THIS AFTERNOON
SHIFT
THEY ARE STILL PUTTING
THEIR CLUB NOTES
IN O.K.

Propaganda notice retrieved from inside pit-head baths *(John Lowe)*

Reported to me tonight that H Harpham and K Butler arrested at Thoresby – cannot confirm at present.

Tuesday 1st May

Morning picket – more ground lost today. Men drifting back. Suspect a variety of reasons:

(a) Beer money
(b) No money
(c) Pressure at home
(d) Greed
(e) Bloody-mindedness

The list could go on. After morning picket up to Berry Hill to frustrate a rally by so-called 'Right to Work' people. The disgraceful aspect was that branch officials conspired with management to organise on such a scale: men were bussed through and in some cases escorted by police to get them there. Pickets meanwhile were turned back by the hundred, miles from their destination, resulting in a great deal of anger and frustration. The demonstration was noisy and abusive with the gulf seemingly wider than ever. Plants from our side showed that men on the dole were among the 'working miners' and were being paid to be there – from where, no one knows. Sessions of stone throwing took place. The size of the police operation had to be seen to be believed: mounted police and dog sections, helicopters circling continually, men who must have numbered close to a thousand plus a number impossible to estimate covering every motorway junction, A road, B road, minor road and cart track. The predictable report by the media gave a grossly distorted picture, especially on the numbers on each side. This was a black day for the Nottinghamshire mining community; this dispute must surely rank alongside 'Spencerism' in the history of the coalfield. On the plus side, our occupation of our Area HQ was a complete success.

Strikers faced by mass of police at Berry Hill *(NUM)*

'Right to work' demonstrators, who were not faced by police *(NUM)*

Provisions passed inside during occupation of NUM offices *(News Line)*

Back to Clipstone for the afters picket – still a drift back. Finally got the information on our two lads in jail: they were in court at Mansfield at 2pm and remanded till June 14th at Worksop. Their story is similar to most cases these days: men are picked out at random, with each new face we encounter seeming to be scalp-hunting.

Wednesday 2 May

Still maintaining forty to sixty picket of our own lads without any difficulty on day shift. It's very wearing though. Odd one still drifting back; have to keep hanging on till something breaks. Letter was drafted and signed by thirty-six asking for a special meeting to permit us to use our own branch banner for the May Day rally in Mansfield. I was informed last night by the welfare secretary that our application for the use of the Lido as a strike centre was refused; also the ladies' use of the village hall was turned down. After picket men moved up to welfare for strike meeting. For our last two strike meetings we have just moved into the lounge as members and then held a meeting. This time the doors were locked; meeting was then held outside on the grass. Still attempting to compile an up-to-date list of members on the picket line; when the hardship cases come in, we'll need some sort of reference. We have made three £10 payments so far. Our £300 from Area has already been severely dented.

Target tonight was Sherwood – four cars sent with no problems. We have received information that BOC[9] drivers will respect a picket at the Area stores along the road; when the police realised our intention, they warned us that it was 'secondary picketing' and that they would arrest. We'll see.

Our plan to toughen our attitude was to occupy the gated pit yard entrance opposite the pit baths, an area hitherto denied us by the police. The men hung back until sufficient numbers were assembled, at which point we moved in and took possession of the area in question. The police were caught totally unawares and their senior 'brass' were hopping mad; their chief inspector went on the warpath, threatening to make wholesale arrests unless we vacated the area immediately. For his troubles he was told that if he arrested one man, he would have to take the lot. This response seemed to throw his brain out of gear and was obviously a new experience for him. He was so used to being obeyed that to have others making the decisions for him presented a problem and, in this instance, he backed off. The result of this episode was that for weeks afterward, they took great care to position their own men in the gateway prior to a change of picket. This we had to count as some sort of success as it helped keep them on their toes and made the point that we were here for a reason. Actions of this kind, it must be said, did nothing to endear us to the police and invariably meant a toughening of their attitude toward us.

May 1st was to see the involvement and duplicity of the Coal Board for what it was. Certain people had 'spontaneously' decided they would hold a 'right to work' demonstration at Berry Hill Park, headquarters of the Nottinghamshire Area of the NUM. In their efforts to encourage the strike-breaking taking place and seemingly off the cuff, the Coal Board decided to allow anyone who was working to take a rest day in order that they might take part in this so-called protest. The whole charade was so transparent as to be sickening.

It was indeed the beginning of a black day in the history of the mining industry in Nottinghamshire. It was also an extremely busy one for we strikers in the county: in common with the rest of the strike centres in Notts, we at Clipstone had been alerted at an early hour to what had been a secret at that point. Accordingly, as soon as the day shift picket ended we went hot-foot to Berry Hill Park to take possession of our Area offices before the roadblocks were in place. Because of our early start, we were able to assemble several hundred strikers in position before the police were organised. Had they been as badly prepared on the county border, we would have had an overwhelming show of support with which to meet those who were opposing us.

Feelings were running very high: I was utterly dismayed by the orchestrated hate that was being directed at us. Some stone-throwing took place and both sides were guilty of this but with the police keeping close watch on our lines, nobody was taking notice of those on the other side of the fence. Of course they took full advantage of this lack of interest in their actions and accordingly the stones fell rather more heavily on our people. This kind of action is always counter-productive and that being the case, nothing the speakers said that day was ever going to improve matters. Looking back, we know it was never the intention of the organisers to listen to reasonable argument.

When the demonstration was finally over and everyone had dispersed, considering that our day had started with an early picket, we still had an afternoon picket to attend, two lads due in court and seven cars of flying pickets to send out for the night shift. During the first three weeks of our involvement, even with our very limited resources, we had still managed to send out more than forty cars full of pickets to other pits. Despite all the dangers of taking part in large pickets, we found the morale of the lads was greatly increased by such involvement. We decided therefore to support 'flyers' as often as our funds allowed.

On the Thursday we had another Clipstone lad arrested, this time at Rufford Colliery. We had sent out four full cars to support the Rufford lads and the police made seven arrests. Once again the 'scalps' were held overnight and bailed by the court the next day.

Thursday 3 May

Alarm as usual at 4am; had to return to bed as I felt really ill. Sent literature down with R Neale; after a sleep I recovered somewhat and went down for the afters picket. Received letters from the Area that had been delivered to the branch secretary: most interesting was that at National Union level they were preparing a dossier on police activities and were requesting details – this we will certainly follow up.

Afternoon spent at DHSS – so much to take in if we are to be in a position to advise on individual claims.

Seven arrested at Rufford night shift picket including one of our lads, A Whibberley. No details yet.

Friday 4 May

Usual fifty on picket line for day shift. I don't think we've lost any more ground and even think there are less men at work, possibly due to rest days. The ladies' section made their first appearance at the picket line when they brought tea, coffee and sandwiches – very much appreciated by the lads. Afternoon picket seemed very slack but we had round about eighty lads turn out. They seem a hardened and keen bunch now. H Harpham went down to pick up A Whibberley from court; charge is 'Threatening behaviour'. Remanded to Mansfield court, June 27th. Details given out for the May Day rally in Mansfield on Monday: we must have a really good turnout. The ladies' section will be walking behind their own banner; as our branch committee have refused us the use of our banner, it seems we must walk behind the ladies' – this we shall do with pride. Complaint by letter from welfare committee about 'rowdy behaviour' by certain elements who had been 'picketing away from the pit'; even if they had their facts right, the whole situation with the welfare committee and the trustees is an absolute disgrace as they obstruct everything that we try to do. After three weeks we are still without a strike HQ or premises for the ladies' section. Smear stories are being spread increasingly, while scare stories such as threatened sack and other downright lies are now a fact of life. I can only keep telling the lads not to be provoked.

Another typical police action at Ollerton last night: a lad was taken when he was nowhere near a picket line; he had been to the fish shop for the family's supper and on returning home was involved in verbal abuse with his neighbours. On appearing in court this morning he was remanded to Lincoln prison for twenty-eight days. Justice is certainly working! The trouble is that it is loaded against us in every department. Sadly, I have to use the word BASTARDS when describing the attitude of many of them; they heel you, prod you, provoke you, then they cordon you off and the 'snatch squad' grabs those who have been fingered. There doesn't need to be an incident for there to be a reason. Frequent interruptions at the Ollerton Area meeting by their lads trying to lobby us over the above incident – a mass demonstration planned for noon on Wednesday 9th at Lincoln jail. Hardship payments set at £3 per head this week – as numbers mount it becomes increasingly difficult to monitor them. Unfortunately time ran out before any form of strategy could be discussed – altogether an unsatisfactory meeting, to say the least.

Monday 7 May

May Day rally at Mansfield: fair turnout but should have been 25,000. Impressive array of branch banners; the disgraceful thing is that the Notts Area ones were outnumbered by the Yorkshiremen's. Scargill as usual was preaching to the converted and I suppose that he will be misreported – or not reported at all. Silverhill lads asking for assistance tomorrow morning for a march on their pit; we said we'd try and send them twenty – it depends on our early turnout. H Harpham and myself met the Cortonwood men and dispersed them throughout the village.

As our applications for supplementary benefit were now due, and in order to be in a position to advise, I paid a visit to the Mansfield offices of the DHSS for a briefing on the subject. Another shock awaited me there: I was taken into an office by a young lady who told me she was a senior member of staff and that she did not believe in such things as strikes. I was speechless at her abrupt manner and made the point that she was not exactly filling me with confidence that our claims would be assessed fairly; her arrogant response was to shrug her shoulders. I came away feeling very depressed, but knew it was something I could not share with the lads just yet: they had problems enough for the present.

May 7th saw the biggest rally and march ever staged in Mansfield. NUM branches came with their banners from every coalfield in Britain to show that the efforts of the Notts strikers were not going unnoticed while trade union branches not connected with mining also came in large numbers to show solidarity with our cause; likewise women's support groups, political groups and a great many individuals disgusted by Thatcher's butchery of the unions. After the speeches were completed and the crowd had started to disperse, the trouble that we did not want was nevertheless forced on us. Many of those present had travelled long distances and needed to locate their transport to get away; the police however herded them on to any coach, regardless of where it came from. They had rightly figured that the lads would resent such an approach and respond accordingly – giving them the green light to step up their own action. A very orderly demonstration by a large number of striking miners quickly became a shambles: areas were cordoned off which stopped people from getting clear, horses were brought in and a large number of people were terrorised and intimidated needlessly. Looking back later, that day was another milestone in our education.

It was not until the next day that we found out two of our Clipstone lads were among the many arrested. One was later charged with riot and, after the dispute ended, remanded to the Crown Court in Nottingham as a part of the 'riot trials' there. After a whole lot of worry and trauma, the police case against the 'Mansfield 55' was finally thrown out of court by the presiding judge.

At the rally we had arranged to meet the Cortonwood Branch: their delegate Mick Carter was to bring a number of their lads who would be staying with us for the week. As this was our first experience of such close working, there was among some a feeling of apprehension as to how this venture would work out. Once the initial settling in was accomplished, however, the reservations were soon dismissed.

Tuesday 8 May

Day shift picket not very well-attended by our own men; it's a good job that the Yorkshire lads are here this morning to boost us. Took a headcount this morning which showed an approximate total of 468 going in. Four cars going to help Silverhill lads; whilst I realise the desperation at some pits, I am reluctant to send men away during the day. However, I've no problem with sending six cars tonight to Sherwood; as reports suggest the night shift has been suspended there, a secondary target of Mansfield has been chosen. A social worker came to the Dukeries to answer individual queries regarding supplementary benefits – he could be very useful to us if and when the number of claimants starts to rise.

Wednesday 9 May
Day shift picket again poorly attended by our own lads; were it not for the Yorkshire lads and a dozen Derbyshire lads who turned up, we would have looked very thin. I want us to assert ourselves against this present supt. (superintendent) but it's impossible without bigger numbers and an earlier start. Our own lads seem to be getting a bit despondent; a boost is badly needed. Barry Smith, Sherwood delegate, informed me that contrary to rumours there would be no buses available for either the upcoming Barnsley or Mansfield rallies; he also told me that no more cash for branches would be paid for seven days owing to the threatened injunction by our friends the scabs.

Thursday 10 May
Slept in this morning and missed the day shift picket – the lads reported a poor turnout by our own men. Something needs to be done as soon as possible to boost them, otherwise the feeling of apathy and frustration will beat us. Hardship cases starting to come in now; single men payments have risen in number but family hardships are now increasing too. The need for the ladies' section to start to function increases daily and any help we can give must be considered a priority – we may have to consider a sit-in, while the same sort of tactics could be employed to secure a strike centre.

Roadblock at White Gates public house this morning again, causing problems even for our own Clipstone workmen as they try to get to the pit for their shift. This sort of thing has got completely out of hand; we seem to have no rights whatsoever, only what the officer on the spot deems to be allowed. A different type of case emerged today. A young lad in court on Tuesday on charges unrelated to the dispute was fined £280, payable at £10 per week; he told the court that, as he was on strike, with no income, he couldn't pay. He was told that if he didn't pay, he would be sent down. I put him in touch with Berry Hill – he was told to seek an application form from the clerk asking for a suspension of the order, then to see solicitors. We learn all the time.

Strike committee meeting at my house, 4.45pm. The need for a strike centre is so urgent that the only way seems to be via a sit-in. Lido facilities decided on for Wednesday morning; trying to obtain a key for a brief period to enable us to make a duplicate. Area stores picket to be established next week and rota to be arranged. Police interpretation – 'black leg' ranks alongside 'scab' and we will be arrested for calling it out. Some of these Little Hitlers seem to be power-mad.

Friday 11 May
Day shift picket reasonable, but no gains made. Morning soup is a very welcome thing. Four cars from Bolsover were ordered away from our line with the threat of arrest despite there being neither trouble nor tension. Contact with DHSS – the wrong rent and rebate forms are being sent out; Mansfield resident has received a form for Newark Council. They admit a 'cock-up' – their words.

Area strike meeting at Ollerton welfare at 10.30am. We drew £63 for single lads hardship; even this will prove insufficient. Many plans to raise cash were aired, most of them speakers going to factories and trade unions – in fact anyone who'll listen and take a collection. Area-wide the hardship is outstripping the cash supply; ladies' sections are springing up all around, but it still takes time to organise and get started. A five-man sub-committee was formed to formulate a tactical campaign, and hopefully they'll keep security tight. Didn't get back until 1.30pm so missed chance to meet the lads after the noon picket; there were many things I wanted to say. Picket report though suggested they were in good spirits. The ladies today had prepared twenty food packs; these were all distributed as soon as possible as they contained some perishables. One case in particular was really desperate and we made a £10 payment – it's becoming clear that before this is over we shall be playing God over the needy, not a role I care for at all. We had figures today showing production for two weeks in April – a 51 per cent drop. What was not stated was that the first set of figures were for a bad week anyhow; if only the media would come clean and tell the truth. They have to be yielding to pressure to be distorting like this. The police actions are even more disturbing: our own lads are now coming back with reports of badly-fitting uniforms, assorted county constabulary badges on the same men, various types of footwear, whole lines with no numbers or numbers covered – and it's being done blatantly.

Sunday 13 May

Meeting this afternoon with officers of the ladies' section – plans formulated for joint action. Problems arranging beds for the Cortonwood boys for this week; the best I can do is three cars. We'll pick them up in Mansfield on Monday at the march. Jim Dowen had a bad meeting with Gedling Colliery official – hang in there, Jim, and don't let him dictate when we are fighting and he is scabbing.

Monday 14 May

Day shift picket about forty. This number is totally ineffectual on the Clipstone picket line, given the geography of the place. Token picket left for the noon shift; the rest of the lads were all heading for the rally – without doubt Mansfield will never see its like again! I feel privileged to have taken part in such a demonstration of SOLIDARITY. However, the whole strategy is wrong: the mass rally achieves no impact where it matters. The tactics, in my opinion, should be marches and rallies in every pit village in Nottinghamshire. So many waverers are there to be convinced and are being allowed to shelter behind petty excuses. Where Clipstone is concerned, I wish to relate and record the following opposition from:

(a) Branch officials who are acting in direct contravention to instructions from the Area Executive
(b) Local miners welfare committee who are obstructing and denying any facility to us
(c) Church authorities who severely limit any facility offered; likewise the local community association
(d) Local Labour councillors who totally oppose us in every way

Clipstone strikers among 40,000 marching in Mansfield *(News Line)*

The day of reckoning must surely come! But it seems to me that after all the sore feet, elation, frustration, bewilderment and anger again experienced, we, as an Area of the NUM, are no further forward today than we were yesterday.

A disturbing report from a privately-owned drift mine at Doe Lea: twenty-nine men, all NUM members, have been sacked with no pay-off of any sort – the price of privatisation that is facing us. Arranged for twelve lads from Cortonwood to be brought in today; they were to be dispersed after the rally, but for the second week running Mick took them back home then sent them on to us the same night. At the meeting point there were only three – I felt badly let down, particularly as so many people from other Areas were looking for accommodation.

Tuesday 15 May
Better turnout for the afternoon shift than the morning one again; no rota for pit gates in operation – a real mess-up. Another incredible instance of how men listen without hearing when being given advice that could be vital to them: A was arrested at the rally yesterday, but this was not reported either to ourselves or to Berry Hill Area HQ until this afternoon – in spite of the fact that he had witnesses present. These men have been told the procedure so many times, I just couldn't believe it … He was in court tonight at 8pm and faced three charges before being bailed; the witnesses have been told to write their statements as soon as possible. Life ain't easy! And the phone bill goes up and up.

Wednesday 16 May

Received two witness statements for A this morning – and also an unrelated one from PP, a laddie who lost part of a leg last year at Mansfield Colliery. On 1st May he was being driven by his wife to the rehabilitation centre at Berry Hill, near the rally, for his daily treatment when they were stopped by the police approximately 600 yards short of his destination. In spite of all their explanations as to his condition and need for treatment, they ignored everything and the lad had to complete his journey on foot – this with an artificial limb and two sticks. He has given permission for this statement to be duplicated and circulated. How many more examples do we need? A headcount this morning showed 564, giving just over 750 for day and afternoon. Everything finalised for the sit-in.

Our women's section had become desperate for somewhere to use as a base. The local community association had allowed them access to their premises, but only to feed the children, while the Church authorities would only allow women and children to be fed in the church institute – our womenfolk were angry and disgusted at such 'Christian charity'. Later, at our strike committee meeting, plans were discussed for a takeover of the facilities at the Clipstone Lido; because of the nature of the times we were living in, stress was laid on the need for secrecy. Within twenty-four hours, one of our own strikers was able to relate in detail to me the entire plan – the ability to keep our mouths closed did not seem to be one of our strong points. As a result, our joint meeting on the Sunday, one that would affect the whole future of the dispute at Clipstone, was restricted to the officers of both committees.

A plan was formulated to take over the Clipstone Welfare Youth Centre and to 'sit in' until we were given a facility to meet our needs. The idea was to gain entry, install a number of men, women and children with enough food, bedding and entertainment to last for a week then sit tight. As this was a whole new area of experience for us all, a great deal of thought was given over to it; and it was to work like a dream.

People, cars and equipment were put in position at 10am and the youth club cleaner was contacted with a story about a lost wrist watch, as we couldn't gain access to the key. Once entry was effected, the emergency doors at the back were opened while cars moved in with everything we needed. Because of the intense police activity in the village, we had set ourselves a ten-minute maximum for the entire operation; for perhaps the first time to date, Lady Luck smiled upon us as we had the place sewn up tight well within that deadline and did not come across any police in the process.

One snag was when the cleaner locked herself in the office and refused to hand over the keys; from there she phoned to the pit for assistance. This meant we had to barricade the doors with anything to hand, not knowing what to expect from the opposition. Within a very short time a Transit van full of police pulled up outside – we fully expected them to attempt to force an entry in an effort to dislodge us, but instead, to our surprise, they just stood back and watched.

When things had settled down some, Jim Dowen and myself made arrangements to see the colliery manager later in the day in an effort to negotiate some kind of a

> deal. At that time we had no way of knowing how the other side were taking the situation we had forced on them. In the meantime, the kids thought it all a great adventure and were really on a high, while the women made themselves busy with the planning of some sort of menu for the following day. No one had ever been involved in anything remotely like this and we were all feeling our way ahead.
>
> With our meeting with the colliery manager arranged for later that day, Jim and myself discussed what our strategy might be; with this in mind, we prepared a list of demands that we intended to put to him.

Wednesday 16 May (continued)

Everything that could be was made secure. Now we wait. Phone calls to the media: Radio Trent and Nottingham put out bulletins which I didn't hear.

Meeting at 2pm with the colliery manager. He was sympathetic to us but was putting forward his 'problems', as he saw them. He had, however, called an emergency meeting of the welfare trustees and committee at 8pm and stated that he would put our case as strongly as he could.

Ladies from Mansfield and Ollerton came for periods during the day and sat in; by evening we were back to our own numbers. No restriction of access all day, with the police just keeping watch and cruising about as usual. Many complaints of the DHSS being slow to process claims; our claims advisor DA came to the sit-in and dealt with some queries. Notts police chief sounding off – the best mouthpiece the Board have had to date. 'Intimidation of families' is the in-phrase; listening to him, every striking miner in the Area could be forgiven for being physically sick.

It was after 10pm before we were invited in to the welfare meeting. The result was this: they have consulted their lawyers and, if we don't vacate the premises, they will seek an injunction to have us removed. However, because they are so big-hearted and don't want any trouble, they will allow us to use the St John's Ambulance Brigade hut until Sunday; at that day's branch meeting, the membership will then decide whether we have a facility or not. That's their offer; it has been decided, therefore, that the sit-in continues – we must make them take the initiative. In the meantime, we have to intensify the coverage by the media. I fear that if I continue at this rate, things are going to crack: from 4am today again, being continually on the go is proving too much of a strain. As I am writing this, the time is 2am. Fourteen ladies arrested today at Silverhill and Sherwood, Scargill's wife [Anne] among them. They are gaining in militancy.

Thursday 17 May

Usual thinly supported picket for day shift. Sit-in still in operation, but the first night's sleep for most has not been very comfortable; no move has been made against us yet. Meeting with the colliery manager where we discussed the problem as fully as we could. He has every sympathy with our position and he is not very happy with the attitude of our worthy(?) NUM members on the committee.

Went back home at 11.30am to have some sleep. In the afternoon Jim Dowen was again in contact with the manager – this time the message was: 'Hang in there, I've an idea I'm turning over in my mind.' There is no doubt he is trying to resolve the problem in our favour; it seems that he's warned 'certain people' and has asked for arrests to be made if we are interfered with. The police superintendent is also reported to be sympathetic to our demands; what an absurd situation it is where management and police are with us and our own NUM people are bitterly against us.

Friday 18 May
Today the Coal Board and the media have taken the 'intimidation of families' charge of [Chief Constable] McLachlan with a vengeance: special plain-clothes squads have been sent into the village to combat this 'menace'. The whole thing has now reached ridiculous proportions; at this rate the police will soon outnumber the local inhabitants. Outraged reaction in the Youth Centre last night to our friend and pensioner Sid Richmond – write his name in letters ten feet high! – being abused: two men accosted him, with one actually kicking him behind the leg. M's reaction was to push them away – very brave. Letter received by the branch secretary today shows how absurd we are making ourselves look: after the National Executive Committee decided earlier this week to suspend the branch elections, they have now reversed that decision. The effect on morale has done nothing to help us, while the confusion caused has given comfort and hope to the 'other camp'. I hope that they know what they are doing.

Saturday 19 May
Third night of the sit-in passed quietly; I half-expected some reaction against us, but it's not happened yet. Radio Trent reporter visited the Youth Centre and interviewed the ladies. Access still no trouble at all, but we must prepare plans for tomorrow in the event that the meeting goes against us – whatever the outcome, we stay.

Strike committee met and decided to concentrate on finance. Decided as follows: with £589 at our disposal, £400 would be spent; single men their £3 allowance then a further £3 if they come picketing; car drivers their £3 petrol allowance for coming to the pit; all others £1 for day picketing; £1 per time on the pit gate rota. Our calculations based on having sixty men on call – if this number is exceeded it eats into our reserve of £189. Our need is to boost the lads; having access to a good dinner after the noon picket has already cheered them tremendously, and we are hoping this extra will do the trick. The efforts of the ladies both providing the meals and during the sit-in have been magnificent and the kids have been just great; hope it doesn't prove for nothing. One incident worth recording today: the vicar's wife brought two men who were looking for a soup kitchen. After a number of questions, the ladies refused to have anything to do with them: they were highly suspicious. Ringers for M?

Sunday 20 May
M's big day! Went into meeting at 9.30am; probably less than 200 attended. The issue we were waiting for was raised under 'correspondence': the only speaker against us was M. The outcome was that the meeting endorsed the branch committee's recommendation that

we be allowed a facility. We must now see the manager to negotiate terms for whatever place we are offered – this in readiness for tomorrow's welfare management meeting. What a climb-down for them! We have to start hitting back now that the smear campaign has started with a vengeance; to this end, we must document and distribute as widely as possible details of the strokes being played against us.

This was the first time we had really been in contact with John Daniels since the start of the dispute, and what we saw, we liked. In direct contrast, M was determined that we would have nothing that would assist our cause. Because of his position he carried a lot of influence which meant we had one hell of a fight on our hands.

The next morning Jim Dowen and myself met once more with the colliery manager; there we presented him with a list of demands to safeguard our position. These he agreed without a moment's hesitation, in marked contrast to certain other people in the village. The next step was to attend a full meeting of the welfare management committee arranged for that same evening.

When we attended, alongside two officers from the women's section, we took great delight in facing these apologies for socialists and hammering out the detail of our victory; the chairman who so had it in for us could do nothing but squirm and submit to all we had demanded. His colliery manager, his branch committee and now his welfare committee had all gone against him; revenge was sweet and we savoured it to the full. Hardship was now building at an alarming rate; expectations for single lads were nil and had to be a priority. We had lads whose parents were threatening to turn them out on the streets unless they returned to work – what an appalling decision for a youngster to have to make! Our problem was that there were so many areas of pressure upon men both married and single that all were fast becoming cases for consideration. At this relatively early stage of the strike, however, pride still prevented many of the families from coming forward: we were only just beginning to learn to confide and share our problems.

Monday 21 May

Still the slow trickle back to work. It's not the greed but the hardship that's driving them back; the pressure that some young families are under is tremendous. With the DHSS slow to make payments and final demands for bills to be settled, we are likely to lose more. It almost seems like a conspiracy against us. One interesting point emerged this morning: M was on Radio Trent today and, from what we hear, he is now having a go at the branch officials because of the number contracting out of political levy. How hypocritical can this man get?

Met the welfare management committee this evening: all our demands were met. We were given the use of the St John's hut for the duration of the dispute with all the safeguards we requested. It was agreed that we vacate the youth premises tonight and complete the transfer tomorrow morning.

Clipstone ladies celebrate procurement of strike HQ; M Hood is at the front *(John Lowe)*

After listening to wild rumours, the youth leader had decided – without bothering to check his facts – that we were 'real baddies'. While waiting for the result, he became very agitated; afterwards, on examining the premises, he totally reversed his opinion and offered us continued use of them.

Tuesday 22 May

Nearly slept in this morning: 5.35am when I arrived on the picket line. After my talk with the men yesterday of the need to tighten our discipline and support on the picket line, it was not surprising that I was the butt of some witty and caustic comments; all good clean fun really. The rains really came this morning; between thirty and forty lads braved the elements. Cleaning the St John's was completed and the transfer took place; from there we went to the noon picket. The police were convinced, I think, that outsiders were present, so numerous were we: they checked car numbers and tax, but were pretty relaxed really.

Wednesday 23 May

Day shift picket greatly improved – usual forty-odd arriving a little earlier and in good voice. The mood of the scabs is changing to outright hostility towards us. Single lad who stood with us yesterday and had just drawn his £3 single allowance went back today after threats from his parents to put him out; others have gone back because of seeming delaying tactics by DHSS with their claims. Our centre really came into its own this morning, with tea and toast ready for the lads after picketing. An inspector tried to cause trouble, threatening to arrest R Hartley for a comment that he made; he backed off when he was told that if he lifted one, he would have to lift thirty.

Ladies made a late start preparing dinner because the cooker was being repaired; old Sid Richmond did a stint 'spud bashing' which was a great help to them. A nice surprise for my wife when she received a basket of flowers delivered to the centre from our next-door neighbours; occasions like this help to lift all the ladies and we appreciated the kind thought behind it. Another policeman this afternoon trying to impress, threatening to 'nick' me when I insisted on inspecting the picket line; he backed off when told to get on with it. While waiting for dinner and afterwards the lads played football; by the time they got home I imagine they were completely knackered. Another lad pressured by the East Midlands Electricity Board for £7 per week. There seems no flexibility with them at all; we should really be pressuring them.

Phone call from Ollerton strike centre: have to meet thirty friends tomorrow morning in White Gates car park – probably a decoy to try and draw the police.

Thursday 24 May

Smallest number yet for day shift picket – about thirty. Headcount showed 480; this will top out something like 520 including deputies and office staff. Breakfast at centre and home to bed for just one hour – luxury! J Strachan and myself arrived at White Gates at 9am; just one car turned up – four Geordie lads from Durham. It does look like a decoy that didn't draw the police.

Afternoon picket shows a lot of strange faces. The four lads I took down were stopped in front of the baths and ordered away under threat of arrest. I took the numbers of the two Gloucestershire Constabulary officers and told them I would be making a complaint; minutes later another group were questioned by an inspector and allowed to stay – this sort of inconsistency just creates tension. At the pit gates, lorries belonging to a firm from Barnsley were inside when a driver approached us. He said yes, they were URT[10], and had authority from the union to fetch coal. We pointed out that he was violating an official picket line. Later in the day Jim Dowen was told by the colliery manager that Supt. G had 'fully investigated' the company and that 'everything was in order with their documents'. The thought of a colliery manager being errand boy for the police, in asking us not to picket these lorries, we consider very funny indeed. Ollerton lads today asked us to provide a car to picket Cottam power station; the idea is for a four-man team from each of four pits to do a six-hour shift daily. As this would cost us around £40 it is beyond our modest means. The national newscasts have been devoid of any mention of this Area today, although I've seen more police vehicles on the move than at any time.

Friday 25 May

Payout at centre after day shift picket – about £230 was distributed. This is the first money the lads have received from us in six weeks, apart from the occasional hardship case. Forum meeting at 10.30am at the TGWU [Transport & General Workers' Union] offices in Nottingham: the South Notts delegates were out to make trouble. The Cotgrave,

Gedling and Newstead people were allowed to make the Forum seem like some ad-hoc committee; Mick McGinty did not help matters with his continual sniping and at times open aggression towards the Newstead delegate. The two National guests seemed to have no idea what living in a Notts mining village is like at the present time. Plans and strategy took no account of the fact that I stand to lose lads on the picket line if money is not forthcoming. Ida Hackett gave a graphic account of the ladies' role in the dispute. The meeting reached a low spot when, despite calls for unity, the South Notts delegates still seemed hell-bent on disruption; at this point I left. I can honestly say I have never felt so disgusted in a meeting, particularly when so much is at stake and the need for unity was never greater.

I visited Cortonwood Miners' Welfare tonight and met many faces that I knew. This encouraged me greatly. The difference is the support forthcoming in South Yorkshire – on the one hand, TOTAL SUPPORT, on the other, our side, a very mixed reception.

Sunday 27 May

Visit to Cortonwood strike HQ this morning – what a difference in attitudes and facilities. I had talks with their officials and was able to make some positive gains, while they also filled the car boot with food for the ladies' section. I visited Silverwood Miners' Welfare this afternoon, only to find it staffed by Cortonwood men; this liaison is another aspect I hadn't expected. The reason for this was that all the available Silverwood men were 'flying', with the target the Sheffield coking plant, Orgreave. The local support has to be seen to be believed.

It would perhaps be appropriate at this point to explain the system and tactics that had developed in Nottinghamshire by this time. Each pit had its own organiser and strike committee; this 'picket manager' attended weekly strike meetings to discuss the requirements and strategy of our own Area. At these meetings he received instructions which were then taken back to be carried out, subject always to the resources of his own pit strike committee.

The officers of the Area strike committee meanwhile were meeting three times each week and making decisions on all matters affecting the strike in Notts. These included such things as the targeting of flying pickets, fundraising, liaising with other Areas and the National leadership – the thousand and one things needed to make the strikers' efforts in Notts effective.

Because we were convinced our phones were being tapped on a large scale, decisions on the targeting of other pits with flying pickets were now being conveyed in code. The code itself was very simple and was changed daily; each branch received only one copy and that was in the keeping of the picket manager. Unless the police had a copy of the current week's code, it was impossible for them to crack. On receiving notification of a target, each picket manager was expected to dispatch as many cars full of pickets as he could afford to send or had available; cash was usually the limiting factor and, although we were drawing money from National level for petrol needs, we were obliged to consider provision through the week for our transport costs with the knowledge that other and bigger bills would soon be coming in.

Just occasionally, Clipstone itself was targeted – the numbers assembled on these occasions gave our lads a terrific boost. To catch the police on the hop was always a satisfying experience, given the hostility they continually displayed to our people. Many large pickets throughout Notts went unreported during the dispute for one obvious reason: the attention of the media was concentrated upon the alleged violence and intimidation perpetrated in the colliery villages by strikers. When one considers the escalation in the numbers that were being arrested and the court practices that had become the norm, there was more than enough material available to satisfy these 'newshounds'; but the fly in the ointment was that it was the striker who was invariably on the receiving end of police violence. That fact alone made it untouchable as far as Fleet Street was concerned.

At about this time, my wife and I were able to make a visit to our eldest daughter and family who lived just outside Rotherham. While there I took the opportunity to visit the strike headquarters of the Cortonwood lads and there I was able to see at first hand the sort of total commitment from their community that was so sadly lacking in Notts; on reflection I realised that in reality the actions of those who were active back home were all the more credible for that. I was able to talk at length with many of their people and, at least for a little while, feel one of the majority.

Although they themselves were in need of all the support they could get, they gave me several telephone numbers of people in various parts of the country who might be of help and support to us. As things turned out, this was to prove the most profitable weekend I could possibly have spent at that time. On reaching home, I was quick to follow up the leads I had been given and within days positive results were forthcoming. Cash had been promised from Sheffield Women Against Pit Closures and the Burnley Miners' Support Group while in addition, the Hackney Trades Council in London had promised to ring us back as soon as they had something positive to report. In little over a week, we were seeing almost daily the fruits of the long telephone sessions; in addition to substantial donations, we were also in line to be adopted as a group by a local Labour Party in Whitby, a Labour constituency in Pendle in Lancashire and a section of staff within County Hall at the GLC in London. As would be expected, the boost to our morale and confidence at that time was beyond measure and as our position was becoming a little more secure, the women could plan ahead with a little more confidence.

Jim Dowen and myself were finding it increasingly difficult to find time to discuss our situation as fully as we would both have liked. His Area responsibilities were taking up almost all of his time and on the few occasions we were together, the opportunity for discussion seldom presented itself. He, for example, as our treasurer, had to be available to the lads whenever he was at the pit; I, on the other hand, always seemed to be busy with the day-to-day arrangements of the strike at Clipstone.

Tuesday 29 May

H Campbell and I went to an open meeting in Ollerton addressed by Henry Richardson to explain the consequences of the injunction that we lost last week; our situation in the law courts seems at great risk. Meeting with the ladies at my house where we agreed to coordinate our efforts in being adopted by outside groups; they also want to man the picket line where possible.

Later picket managers meeting at Ollerton; strategy discussed, but cannot be described here due to the secrecy involved. Petrol money set at 9p per mile; the Forum will pay picketing money, beginning tomorrow.

Wednesday 30 May

Disturbing events from Blidworth recently: the police action, in their search for Yorkshire-men, seems to know of no limits to their authority. There are eyewitness reports of enter-and-search; threats to arrest local inhabitants who have left their premises; and breaking in through the door of the women's action centre, thus terrorising women and children who were eating a meal. Where can it end?

Unfortunately only one car was sent to Bentinck target today. Our organisation is too lax; we have to lift the men and insist on the discipline and support of everybody. For this reason, the centre has to be open much earlier.

P.S. The special plain-clothes squads ordered into the village are reported to have adopted the name Fast Action Response Teams – until they realised the initials.

Thursday 31 May

Four cars, seventeen men, away today to Sherwood. Large picket with no problems reported; B Herbert, however, had two tyres let down. Sid Richmond, our pensioner friend, brought his usual £5 donation; he really is a source of encouragement to us all. A full picket meeting was called for 2pm but for the second time it had to be cancelled after a call from Ollerton to a picket managers' meeting. Mansfield ladies' section are having a delivery tomorrow stated to be £3,000 worth of food. We are to supply two ladies, two cars and six lads to assist unloading, recording and dispersing. Phoned Berry Hill re: rally in London next Thursday. Was told that National are prepared to pay for six buses down there from Notts.

On ITV tonight Jim Hood[11] and the Ollerton strike centre were featured: I only caught the last ten minutes but was impressed by his performance. Sections of the media seem to be changing their attitude to our cause.

I was informed later that this particular programme was very one-sided. It seems that the last bit I caught was the only favourable comment in the whole show. SO WHAT'S NEW?

Notes

1. George Spencer, Labour MP for Broxtowe, formed an openly scab union in Nottinghamshire during the 1926 General Strike which was in cahoots with the Conservative Government of the day
2. Famous socialist author from United States
3. Henry Richardson, NUM Notts Area General Secretary
4. Ray Chadburn, NUM Notts Area President

5. Transport and General Workers' Union (now Unite)
6. Son of M
7. Miners welfare trustees' chairman, Labour councillor and ex-branch secretary
8. Brief, victorious pay strikes for the miners which resulted in the downfall of Edward Heath's Tory Government
9. British Oxygen, an industrial gas company
10. United Road Transport Union
11. Chairman of Notts Miners' Forum and present Labour MP for Lanark & Hamilton East

PART TWO

JUNE–AUGUST 1984

Friday 1 June

Target today was Calverton, as it was their branch elections. It seems there was a leak, or the police anticipated well: they were there on a massive scale and most did not get through. Our lads did, but were turned back repeatedly even when on foot. The promise of help from the Burnley support group arrived in the form of a £100 cheque; better still, a call from them this morning to the effect that we have been adopted by Whitby for support. A call from Sheffield ladies last night to say they were also putting a cheque for £100 in the post for the ladies' section. There are others putting feelers out for us. Bill Bush[1] of the GLC also wants us to call on him at County Hall if we are able to get to the rally in London.

Picket payout amounted to 50p per picket – disappointment for the lads who were hoping for a £1 payment. Single lads payments have now stopped and this has upset some, notably M Hood, who had a real go at me: this lady is beginning to get right up my nose. The rule now is clear: come and picket and get something or stay home and get nowt.

Saturday 2 June

Demonstration at Ollerton was very well-supported; the police estimated the crowd at 3,000. All the speakers, including Tony Benn, were very well received. The message, loud and clear to those scabbing, was: 'With you we can win, without you we will win!' It becomes clearer every day that the support outside our county being turned towards us is awe-inspiring. In the face of so much friendship, one feels humble, proud and elated. I only hope that this feeling rubs off on all our lads.

A call this afternoon from a Mr Tim Ormerod of Pendle Labour Party, Lancashire. He was seeking information regarding Clipstone and our ladies' group. His members are paying a 50p-per-week levy; he still needs to consult his officers, but the signs look good for us to benefit.

Sunday 3 June

Called Bill Bush this morning: he told me that as County Hall has many sections, with some sizeable ladies' sections amongst them, the signs look good for support from there; they are keen to meet our representatives next Thursday in order to put our case. Had a call from a lady in Mansfield offering to make a donation to the ladies, which tied up the telephone for quite a while; however, these people not connected with mining who have so much sympathy for our cause are amongst the best advocates that we could have at this time. Above all, we must <u>never</u> forget our friend from Burnley, IL, who has put us in touch with so many contacts.

Monday 4 June

Target day shift was Thoresby – one car, five men only. Our own picket sparsely attended. Luckily again lads from other pits who didn't beat the Thoresby roadblocks boosted our numbers somewhat. We had another batch drift back today, with the usual excuses. Cock-up when N and H Campbell didn't turn up with the centre key; I had to knock them up to get the damn thing. It now stays in my possession.

Second target today was Clipstone Colliery. What a picket! There must have been 300–400. Did we give the police something to think about! After a couple of surges against them, they brought out the horses; on this occasion, they were not used aggressively against us – the amount of traffic on this particularly busy road persuaded them to hold back a little. We had occupied the small green and the pavement in front of the pit canteen. The scabs still went in, except one – what an expenditure of energy for one man. Luckily no arrests were made. After what happened, with all the problems that we caused them, this was surprising.

A lot of loose talk has been going around the village which I bitterly resent: the gist of it was that John Lowe had been telling certain people in advance the target for a flying picket hit. This is totally untrue. My feelings this afternoon were that with my integrity being called into question, I no longer wanted the job; we'll see how things go for the next day or two.

Policeman supervises mass picket at Clipstone *(News Line)*

Tuesday 5 June

Police smarting from yesterday. That much is obvious from today's reaction: the inspector coming down heavy and refusing to give answers. After my reaction the superintendent, his boss, became angry and threatened to arrest me for 'intimidating lorry drivers by having a notebook in my hand'. How bloody laughable can you get? I told him that I was going to monitor all vehicles going in all day. This was done by the lads picketing the pit gates and he seems to have backed off.

Two cars were sent to Rufford: reports later of a large picket. As there was no through-flow of traffic to complicate the situation, the lads were hit from the front and when many tried to get out of the way they were hit from behind with the horses. A whisper from 'over the wall' states that even with the drift back to work, production is still down by almost two thirds; have not been able to verify this. Desperate cases mentioned again tonight; ladies have put up a list for food parcels which they cannot fill. They are contacting Mansfield to have them made up. Bill Bush has laid on a room with a cup of tea at the GLC for after the march; something like sixty people have pledged support through what he calls the 'Friends of Clipstone' group.

Wednesday 6 June

Figures for day shift picket seem to have settled at just under forty. I would like to see many more, but if we hold this we can manage. Flyers sent from my home this morning at 9am – four cars to Hucknall. Police harassed the pickets, chasing them off and lifting. Our lads found cover and avoided trouble.

Full strike meeting was held after dinner. The men were told quite firmly what the financial situation was and, after a few moans and grumbles, the facts were accepted without protest. Jim Dowen helped in this: I was prepared to meet the argument and to overrule any dissent, while Jim instead explained fully the wider efforts being made, topping this with congratulations for their efforts – wise and clever old bugger.

At home later a call from Northern Ireland, of all places – a Mr Hamilton of the GMBATU.[2] After giving him the background to the situation, he promised a cheque for £100.

Thursday 7 June

Larger than usual day shift picket due to the trip to the demo in London today. There were no incidents and everyone was in good spirits.

> The rally in London was a National event with a march and speeches to be held in the Jubilee Gardens close by County Hall. This was to be followed by a lobby of Parliament where we would have the opportunity to meet with those of our supporters in Westminster who were not afraid to put their heads above the battlements. The coach duly arrived at 6.40am and we were on our way, full of enthusiasm; the journey down was something of an anti-climax after the anticipation that had built over the preceding days. Not until we stopped at a service station did

we realise the enormity of the day: here we were able to mingle freely with colleagues from all over Britain and – for a change – without a policeman in sight. We felt part of the human race once again, and how we enjoyed the feeling.

From there onward there was an ever-increasing number of vehicles: 'Coal not dole' was the message proclaimed in noisy fashion throughout. We had been told to assemble at King's Cross in readiness for an 11am start but, by the time we arrived, it was 11.20am and the march was well on its way. So many were there, however, that we were able to join the back of the column with many thousands more still to come behind us. What an atmosphere to savour, and what a tremendous reception we received from those who had assembled to watch. The occasion had a welcome feeling of carnival after the tension we had suffered of late and even the police – at that stage – seemed relaxed. Alas, we should have known better – the leopard does not change its spots quite so easily.

At a certain point along the route, three of the lads were snatched from the centre of the column and taken away to Bow Street police station, while the first half of the march carried on, unaware of what had happened. The rest of us halted and refused to continue until the three were brought back and restored to their place in the column. It was obvious that these were deliberate police tactics, part of their strategy for the day: two helicopters circled continually, surely filming proceedings, while there was a camera mounted directly above us. We realised we were expected to retaliate, thus giving them an excuse for stepping up their own action, while also providing the media with its anti-strike film for the day.

Not for the first time, the police had miscalculated. We maintained our discipline, refusing to move until the lads were brought back; this went on for one and a quarter hours, with the Law threatening us with everything short of transhipment to a penal colony. Bus drivers left their buses full of passengers to stand with us in unity; onlookers encouraged us to stand our ground. The senior police 'brass' present were beside themselves with anger as their 'orders' were ignored.

To take the heat out of the situation, a brass band that was marching with us came forward and played an impromptu selection that kept both marchers and onlookers entertained. While all this was happening, a barrister who was marching with us had gone down to the Bow Street 'nick' and secured the release of the three lads, who were then brought back by the police and placed as requested at the head of the column.

This was considered by everyone to be a very significant victory for us and spirits were never higher.

Thursday 7 June (continued)

From this point the police escort increased continually: the side streets were packed with them – they seemed to be crawling out of the brickwork. We finally arrived at the Jubilee Gardens area to find a solid mass of police blocking the road; the reason for this escaped us as we were almost at the end of our march. The band leading us then did a most unusual thing: they began playing again and marched at the police roadblock. This was followed by a push from the rest of the march, who didn't know what was happening in front: women and children were involved at the front and I was told later that some of the kids were injured. We had just decided to get our ladies out of the way when all hell broke loose: the police were rushing forward in twos and threes and grabbing people and throwing them to the floor; their arms were being forced up their backs in the most brutal and painful way; they were being grabbed by the hair. And again, a camera just happened to be mounted immediately above the scene: I was in no doubt that the police had picked their spots for a confrontation. There seemed to be thousands of them. Missiles were thrown by our people, mainly empty pop cans and plastic bottles; they would not cause much damage, but certainly gave the other side an excuse to escalate the situation. At this point we realised that one of our ladies, M Hood, was missing. Having collected the rest of our party, we shepherded them into the County Hall building. What a surprise awaited us! We were taken through to a waiting reception, even though we were an hour late – tea, biscuits, hot sausage rolls and fruit juice were laid out for us. When everyone was settled and rested, Bill Bush welcomed us and spoke of the positive support behind us; an envelope containing £200 was handed over to the ladies and a number of bags and boxes containing food were also given. Our thanks seemed inadequate in light of such generosity. Meanwhile, we could watch the whole scene as the march on Parliament crossed Westminster Bridge: another rough confrontation took place, the two sides coming together in what could have been some medieval battle, banners flying and police wading in; so much for our legal right to assemble and demonstrate, and for putting our case to the public at large and our Parliamentary representatives at Westminster. About that time we heard that M had been arrested; the party was started on its way back while Jim and myself arranged for T Hood to stay behind. Back at the bus T McGowan was missing so we had to set out without him; I spent time at the service station phoning London 'nicks', worried about him, with no joy. We arrived home at 9.30pm. With chance to sit and look back, I am really proud of the way that our lads conducted themselves: they could quite easily have become involved in the trouble, but kept their heads and sought to protect the ladies. What I have seen today has filled me with disgust for the so-called forces of law and order: when senior officers are openly calling us scum using loudhailers, when women and children are being abused and threatened, when there is no effort to disguise the intention of their violent tactics, we have every reason to fear for whatever freedom we have left in Notts.

When M Hood was released, County Hall got her and her husband to a train station, with T calling me from Nottingham at 10.10pm. Jim Dowen went at a minute's notice to fetch them. The story of her experience with the police was horrific: she was swore at, called a cow, told that they were running a 'Police State' in England; she was handled in a most appalling manner, by the neck and then with both arms forced up her back. Open hostility towards miners I can just about accept – but when it is directed at their families, I will never accept it. Women in Northern Ireland do not get the treatment meted out to some of ours. T McGowan also turned up later, having got on the Rufford coach; silly bugger me for panicking about him. Note: on arriving home my wife and I found the sort of letter that I wouldn't wish on my worst enemy. The foul and twisted minds that sent these out, unsigned of course, are not worthy of concern on my part. It did, however, upset my wife for a while.

Striker arrested outside Parliament *(News Line)*

What a load of codswallop, Cooking meals for striking miners! Cooking meals for idle bleeders who are no doubt supping and smoking in the pubs out of the child allowance. I'd give them bugger all for money, I'd like to spit in the bloody soup. They can go to work and earn £65 a week, working about 4 hours a day and they want charity. Let the women go on the game they'd get more. The Government should stop all payments and call out the troops and shoot the bloody lot. My wages this week were £136·6ᵖ I have enclosed the 1ᵖ for your fund, you won't put much out of that in your own pocket.
(You scrounging bastards)

Working Miner.

P.S. SCARGILL GETS £26,000 A YEAR. YOU SUCKER

Hate mail sent by 'working miner' to John Lowe, one of several *(John Lowe)*

Friday 8 June

The alarm this morning felt like an electric shock. We need to make contact with some of the lads we are not seeing on the picket line – we know we have lost a lot back to work that have not come forward to us. The trouble is they isolate themselves and, when the pressures arise, they have no back-up. Jim is having a honeymoon this week at Mablethorpe – good luck to him, he's earned his break.

Monday 11 June

Picket down to twenty-six today – it must be the lowest yet. Our new supt. from this Bedfordshire mob, whose name we don't even know yet, has started off in a very prickly manner, even banning the word 'rubbish'. Arrangements for M Hood's court appearance in London tomorrow took up part of the morning.

NATIONAL COAL BOARD   CLIPSTONE COLLIERY

North Nottinghamshire Area

                                       MANSFIELD
                                       NOTTS. NG21 9AR
Our ref   *Your ref*   Telephone : Mansfield 22148

                                       8th June, 1984.

Dear Mr. Lowe,

    I note that you are still absent from work despite the fact that
the High Court has ruled that men at work in Nottinghamshire are perfectly
in order and have not broken any rules of the Union nor can they be
disciplined for breach of Union rules relative to the current dispute.

    You will be aware that since the Spring Bank Holiday there has been
a return to work by a large number of men previously absent for one reason
or another. You are therefore becoming one of a decreasing number of men
not at work.

    In order to operate this pit efficiently and economically, we require
the presence of every man on books. I therefore ask you to seriously
consider your position and let me know when you intend to return to your
employment.

    I would appreciate an early reply as I need to know your position
in planning the future manning of the Colliery.

                    Yours sincerely,

                    J.A. Daniels,
                    Colliery Manager.

Letter sent out to strikers by management *(John Lowe)*

Tuesday 12 June

The police are very sensitive: they are threatening the lads with arrest for the silliest of
reasons. We shall have to start prodding back a bit harder; we are sick of being pushed
about. Flyers were away to Mansfield rather early, but a very large picket estimated at
1,000 was nevertheless there by the time they arrived; eleven were arrested, including
A Snaith. He will be in court at 7pm tonight.

```
11th June, 1984


TO:   THE COLLIERY GENERAL MANAGER



Dear Sir,

In reply to your letter dated 8th June, 1984, re our absence from
work, we should like to point out that we also have not broken any
Union rules.  Our Union states we are not to cross any picket lines during
the OFFICIAL STRIKE which covers the Nottinghamshire Area, even though
a small percentage of miners have taken out and won a High Court order
allowing them to work.

We realise that a number of men have returned to work for various
reasons, but we believe that to ensure a safe future in mining, we
are supporting the 87% of men who are fighting for their jobs.

Pit closures are inevitable in all areas, and this covers management
as well as men, to which we are sure you will fully agree.

Under the circumstances, you will understand that until this dispute is
settled to everyone's satisfaction, we shall remain on official strike
with the majority of miners.  Hopefully, it will soon be over and then
we shall all return to work immediately.

Yours faithfully,



          John E Lowe


          JOHN E LOWE
```

Standard reply sent to colliery *(John Lowe)*

Two haulage firms were reported to Barnsley today, one from Barnsley and the other from Sheffield. Maybe we'll get the same reaction from the colliery as last time; good to put the cat among the pigeons, at least. Fundraising arranged for two of our lads to go with two Ollerton lads to Oxford tomorrow; H Harpham went yesterday to Peterborough for the week. His court appearance comes up on Thursday so he'll have to come back in the morning.

Wednesday 13 June

Picket numbers again down. Less than thirty coming at present. No incidents and no progress. Area strike centre supposed to be manned from 4.30am onwards, as I understand. I couldn't get a reply until 5.25am when trying to get my code. I need to be able to make contact before I leave home, or they phone through so early they get my wife out of bed. Not good enough! Took up PC's case with DHSS re: refusal of special diet for his young daughter and travelling expenses when she was in hospital. The way this lad has been treated is shameful: we've been promised different things and now he has to write in again, to Nottingham this time. Hassle all the way.

K Butler and R Hartley sent to Ollerton at 12pm to be instructed by lawyer JB on how to take statements when the need arises; one car load also sent at 2pm to be instructed in our legal rights – what to do and not to do if arrested. This advice is very badly needed in light

Strikers' procedure following arrest *(John Lowe)*

ADVICE ON ARREST

As soon as possible you or your friends or family should contact the strike committee for the area in which you were arrested.

AT THE POLICE STATION:

<u>DO</u>

* ask for bail. The police must give you bail or take you to a magistrates court for them to consider bail within 24 hours (48 hours at weekends).

* tell the police that you want to make a telephone call.

* check the police list of your property and sign immediately below the last item to prevent additions.

* memorise the name or number of any policeman who threatens or assaults you.

* demand to see a senior officer if any of your requests are refused.

UNTIL YOU HAVE SPOKEN TO A LAWYER OR STRIKE COMMITTEE OFFICIAL:

<u>DO NOT</u>

* speak to the police or make a written statement about the picket and the circumstances of your arrest. You have a right to silence.

* agree to give your fingerprints or take part in an identity parade. You have a right to refuse unless a court orders you to.

* agree to be photographed. The police may photograph you anyway but they have no right to use force.

AT COURT:

UNTIL YOU HAVE SPOKEN TO A LAWYER OR STRIKE COMMITTEE OFFICIAL YOU SHOULD:

* plead not guilty to all charges.

* ask for legal aid. You are entitled to legal aid if you need legal advice and cannot afford to pay a solicitor.

* ask for unconditional bail. The magistrates can only refuse bail or impose conditions if they have a good reason to think that:

  1 you will fail to turn up at court for your trial   <u>or</u>

  2 you will commit an offence whilst on bail   <u>or</u>

  3 you will interfere with witnesses.

  If you will not accept bail conditions imposed by the magistrate, you may be kept in custody.

National Coal Board
Hobart House, Grosvenor Place, London SW1X 7AE

CHAIRMAN
Ian MacGregor

June, 1984

Dear Colleague,

<u>YOUR FUTURE IN DANGER</u>

I am taking the unusual step of writing to you at home because I want every man and woman who has a stake in the coal industry to realise clearly the damage which will be done if this disastrous strike goes on a long time.

The leaders of the NUM have talked of it continuing into the winter. Now that our talks with them have broken down this is a real possibility. It could go on until December or even longer. In which case the consequences for everybody will be very grave.

Your President talks continually of keeping the strike going indefinitely until he achieves "victory".

I would like to tell you, not provocatively or as a threat, why that will not happen however long the strike lasts.

What this strike is really about is that the NUM leadership is preventing the development of an efficient industry. We have repeatedly explained that we are seeking to create a higher volume, lower cost industry which will be profitable, well able to provide superior levels of earnings while still being able to compete with foreign coal. To achieve this, huge sums of money are being invested in new equipment; last year it was close to £800 million and we expect to continue a similarly high rate of investment in the years ahead. Our proposals mean, short term, cutting out some of the uneconomic pits and looking for about 20,000 voluntary redundancies – the same as last year. The redundancy payments are now more generous than ever before for those who decide not to take alternative jobs offered in the industry.

However long the strike goes on I can assure you that we will end up, through our normal consultative procedures, with about the same production plans as those we discussed with your representatives on 6th March last.

But the second reason why continuing the strike will not bring the NUM "victory" is this: in the end nobody will win. Everybody will lose – and lose disastrously.

Many of you have already lost more than £2,000 in earnings and have seen your savings disappear. If the strike goes on until December it will take many of you years to recover financially and also more jobs may be lost – and all for nothing.

I have been accused of planning to butcher the industry. I have no such intention or desire. I want to build up the industry into one we can all be proud to be part of.

But if we cannot return to reality and get back to work then the industry may well be butchered. But the butchers will not be the Coal Board.

You are all aware that mines which are not constantly maintained and worked deteriorate in terms of safety and workability.

AT THE PRESENT TIME THERE ARE BETWEEN 20 and 30 pits which are viable WHICH WILL BE IN DANGER OF NEVER RE-OPENING IF WE HAVE A LENGTHY STRIKE.

This is a strike which should never have happened. It is based on very serious misrepresentation and distortion of the facts. At great financial cost miners have supported the strike for fourteen weeks because your leaders have told you this .....

> That the Coal Board is out to butcher the coal industry.
> That we plan to do away with 70,000 jobs.
> That we plan to close down around 86 pits, leaving only 100 working collieries.

IF THESE THINGS WERE TRUE I WOULD NOT BLAME MINERS FOR GETTING ANGRY OR FOR BEING DEEPLY WORRIED. BUT THESE THINGS ARE ABSOLUTELY UNTRUE. I STATE THAT CATEGORICALLY AND SOLEMNLY. YOU HAVE BEEN DELIBERATELY MISLED.

The NUM, which called the strike, will end it only when you decide it should be ended.

I would like you to consider carefully, so we can get away from the tragic violence and pressures of the mass pickets, whether this strike is really in your interest.

I ask you to join your associates who have already returned to work so that we can start repairing the damage and building up a good future.

Sincerely,

Ian MacGregor

Ian MacGregor denies industry is under threat *(John Lowe)*

of a new publication just issued, 'A State of Siege', a report to the Yorkshire NUM by two NALGO[3] members. The code is working a treat and can't be broken – I think we're finally giving them the runaround, and not before time.

Thursday 14 June

The two in court today were again remanded with bail conditions remaining in force – i.e. not allowed near a picket line or pit – in spite of protest. This is the authorities' way of grounding lads who have not been found guilty of any offence. The disgusting thing is that the courts are dancing to the police's tune. We have virtually no protection until the powers being used against us have been curbed. Talks broke down today between ourselves and Maggie's puppet. Verdict? Predictable.

Friday 15 June
Afternoon picket: I did not attend. My back trouble kept me at the centre. With Jim tied up at a meeting in Barnsley till the afternoon and having to hand his cash and book over, with some of last week's picket money still to be paid out and petrol money for this week also outstanding, I felt a little snowed under; a certain amount of depression has set in with the fatigue. Later, two of the lads came to see me demanding to know why I hadn't been able to conjure up a bus for the Yorkshire miners' gala at Wakefield! Just in time, Jim turned up to rescue me from an argument. Currently on our way to a public meeting in Wellingborough, where Jim and his wife H are due to speak.

After the day he'd had, Jim spoke very well and was well-received by a better-attended meeting than I expected. Elsie, my wife, admitted she was almost moved to tears by H's speech. A collection taken realised £140, which really surprised me considering we were in a depressed area with a high unemployment percentage. We arrived home at 1am, very tired but well-satisfied.

Joe Green, Yorkshire picket, was killed by a lorry on the picket line today. Number two. How many more?[4]

Saturday 16 June
The most exciting call so far came from Tim Ormerod in Pendle today: he was asking for speakers for next Friday and within two hours had fixed up digs for two couples, put together a full programme for Saturday and made a start on Sunday's programme. This seems a golden opportunity to finance our Area fund while also supporting our own ladies group: these people are anxious to identify with a particular colliery village. At this point I had better stop writing, as a two-and-a-half-litre bottle of Mansfield Bitter does not lend itself to an accurate or legible report.

Monday 18 June
Rent-a-mob this week come from Bath: they seem a bit more easygoing than the edgy, miserable sample of the last two weeks. H Harpham going back to Peterborough today and taking D Anderson with him; his team last week made £500. Our own lads now have a chance for a change of scene plus the experience of meeting with and talking to a range of different types of people.

Stories coming in of the 'horror of Orgreave'; there, for the past three weeks, the lads have been subjected to the same kind of brutal treatment that we experienced in London. Scores of people have been charged down and injured. Scargill in hospital is the latest; it's about time that more of our people in office identified with the lads on the picket line. Our time will come – but being on the inside in Notts, trying to hang on, is very wearing. We'd far rather be on the outside and solid, trying to get in.

David Gareth Jones from the Yorkshire Area had died at the beginning of the strike at Ollerton in questionable and distressing circumstances. In June, Joe Green, another Yorkshire miner, was killed on the picket line. Incidents like these made very little impact on either newspaper reporting or television: they were not the stories they were paid to look for. If the lads had been 'working miners', it would have been a whole new ball game: the media needed scab victimisation stories to lend respectability to their editorial commentary on events.

Fundraising of necessity was really taking off throughout the country, with women's support groups and strike committees sending speakers all over the place: M Hood travelled on behalf of the Notts women central committee both at home and on the continent while Clipstone strikers went to London, Norwich, Liverpool, Grimsby, Peterborough, Whitby, Northern Ireland, anywhere they were sent, to raise money to finance the strike. At any time before, these same people would have ridiculed any forecast of their involvement in public speaking or negotiation of anything larger than a family budget. There were no questions or arguments – the need was great and they just went. These lads of ours were tremendous.

The stories coming through of the 'Battle of Orgreave' made most of our experiences to date pale by comparison. The lads were angered by it. A lot of Notts lads managed to get to Sheffield and the Orgreave picket, but as a strike group in Notts we were not in any position to organise anything outside the agreed strategy of the Area. With cash for petrol in short supply and our many commitments locally, we could not send our meagre resources elsewhere, much as we would have liked to involve the lads in this operation. If we'd had access to our own Notts Area funds, as was the case where the strike was solid, we may well have been in a position to operate differently.

When, later, it was possible to analyse the actions of the police, the photographic evidence showed just how far removed they were from the public perception of the time – and this for an industrial dispute alone. From Orgreave until the end of the strike, we could see how it was used as an opportunity by the authorities to test the efficiency of their public order strategy without fear of repercussions from the public.

Tuesday 19 June

After talking with lads from Thoresby, Mansfield and Bilsthorpe when they've used our centre I don't feel quite so bad about the seeming lack of support from certain of our own lads: their organisation seems to fall far short of ours. In better spirits for the day shift today; still only twenty-six but morale is high. Anger rather than depression seems to be the reaction. A lot of shamed faces are going through. The other bastards are so brazen in their attitude that a reaction could be forgiven; by me, at least.

Wednesday 20 June

Oh, for a big picket! We are very short of cars at this time: only one for the flyer tonight, target Bentinck. Yorkshire lorries still coming in regularly. Seem to have been running around a lot today and getting nowhere.

Thursday 21 June

The supt. this week has not attempted to make any contact all week and neither have his inspectors. I prefer it that way – I am suspicious of them all. An incident today illustrates why I feel justified in my attitude: a lorry driver at the noon picket on his way out of the gates has continually stuck his fingers up at the lads. Today he did the same again, telling the nearest of them to 'bollocks'. This was immediately in front of a sergeant and two constables. They agreed, when asked, that if our lads had done the same, they would have taken action. On being asked why they did not do so with the driver, I was told: 'Ask my governor.'

We seem to have reached a position now where our contacts have been exhausted and we rely on certain ones for repeat support; however, we still have every reason to be hopeful. The lads in Whitby have run into difficulties with the law in their efforts to collect on the streets; it's a hard sell, but they are remaining optimistic and have collected £100 for the Notts Miners' Forum and £80 for the ladies so far.

Friday 22 June

Arrived at 6.30pm for a Labour Party meeting at Nelson and Pendle; Jim spoke first, followed by myself then H. From there we were taken to a Labour club in Burnley where we met IL, our old friend and contact; we were also introduced to their new Euro MP. One more call for a pint then we were taken on to our digs: our hosts MH, a probation officer, and his wife A, a schoolteacher, have a background and lifestyle somewhat different to our own – but we'll make out all right.

Saturday 23 June

Our day began at 10am with a collection at the Co-op in Nelson – a dead loss as far as cash and goods are concerned. We were only allowed at the back entrance from the car park. Leaflets advertising Sunday's meeting were handed out, along with copies of 'The Miner'. The second Co-op was a little better, with more chance to talk to people and a more positive response.

Saturday evening was really something else: a barge trip on the top of the Pennines. The three-hour trip, with plenty to drink, showed us the type of character that Tim Ormerod is: he raffled a miniature flame lamp, auctioned a helmet and made a collection, from a limited number, amounting to £69.

Sunday 24 June

Met a couple of local lads in the afternoon that we saw briefly on Friday: both Jim and myself had both given some thought to these, who seem to us so isolated even with 100 in Burnley on strike – they seem to have no organisation. I think we both felt a little guilty that we were fundraising on their own doorstep after hearing of their problems. At the planned meeting, Jim and H spoke for us among local Labour councillors and the Euro MP: the end result was a cheque for £900 plus a boot-load of food. Quite a weekend; in actual fact, it came as a bloody shock. Included in this was a donation from an old lady for £300; the lump I felt was, I think, felt by us all. After a farewell cup of tea we departed and got home by 6.30pm to learn of the result of the branch meeting decision on our application for use of the banner: the lads did us proud, but only by one vote.

Monday 25 June
Police still maintaining last week's improved image. For how long, I wonder? Their numbers are way down compared with previous weeks. The scabs are now hanging on for their holiday cash. Two cars, nine men, sent to West Burton power station. Mid-morning I went to Berry Hill for two or three items, but that was the extent of my involvement today: the rest was spent on private family business.

Tuesday 26 June
Day shift picket as usual. Today is one I want to forget; things were said that would have been better left unsaid.

Wednesday 27 June
I left for the centre around 10am and had the shock of my life: the avenues were alive with Yorkshiremen. Some of them managed a quick cup of tea at the centre, but we had to get them to the pit quickly. I took one large group down Church Road, solely to keep them off the main road; minutes after I left, the centre of the village was alive with police. They were worried sick: Transits full of them were harassing and threatening all over the place, but my group managed to get to the pit unchallenged. I set up the picket line and the Yorkshire lads were slowly shepherded along to the 'green' with pushes and threats; after a short while a group moved forward to establish themselves in a more realistic position. I moved forward with them, with the intention of checking our lads along the front of the baths; this is a regular practice I have followed right through the dispute. At this point a number of police moved in front of us and started pushing us, telling us to go back. The men moved back slowly to their original position whilst I stood my ground because of my intention to check the line. A local constable amongst them was saying: 'Mr Lowe, go back please.' I asked repeatedly what I was doing wrong and, if I was causing an obstruction, to tell me how and where. My questions were ignored while the officers continued to jostle me. I sat on the grass, telling them I was refusing to move; two grabbed me, one on each side, by the arms and pulled me to my feet. I pulled back and one of them must have lost his footing because the one to the left of me fell, pulling me down with him which in turn pulled the one on the right down on top of me. What followed then is something of a nightmare. I was conscious of at least three other officers on the floor holding me down; one said 'put the handcuffs on him' and I then received a clip to the right side of my jaw followed by a forearm brought viciously down across my throat. The forearm was then pressed hard on to my throat and the handcuffs placed on to my right wrist; I was turned over on to my stomach, with the pain from the handcuff being used as an 'incentive' to comply. Once on my stomach my left wrist was also handcuffed, this one being squeezed on even harder: such was the pain, I called out: 'You bastards, you bastards.' I was then picked up bodily in a face-down position and carried to the 'Maria',[5] which was standing conveniently just a few yards away.

Six policemen deal with John Lowe while a seventh looks on *(John Lowe)*

John Lowe carried to mobile detention vehicle *(John Lowe)*

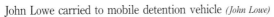

Wednesday June 27th 1984 was the day when my luck finally ran out. By mid-morning it was plain that we were in for a sizeable crowd for the afternoon picket; we had no prior warning of the influx as we were privy only to the plans of our own Area. We got most through to the pit, by which time the police had assembled an impressive array of force opposite; and still the Yorkshire lads kept arriving.

After my arrest I was ordered to sit down. An attempt to photograph me with a Polaroid camera was made which I resisted vigorously – all they managed was a picture of the top of my head. The questioning began immediately; I refused to cooperate, except to confirm my name and address, which they knew anyhow. By this point, I was locked inside one of the cells of this mobile cell block – and, left alone, there I waited.

The reader should understand the authorities' policy during this period: namely that the actions of the pickets played little or no part in determining the number of people arrested at any given point. Their priorities were governed by how much space was available in the cells back at the 'nick'; the more they could accommodate, the more 'scalps' they would take and the greater the intimidation they were able to wield. Some of the senior police officers were the worst offenders in this regard – faceless individuals who relished the power they were allowed on the ground.

The wagon imprisoning me was driven into the pit yard and parked up to await further passengers, which were not long in coming: two Yorkshire lads were followed by J Strachan, one of our own strikers. By that time my wrists were bleeding from the handcuffs; with my hands still behind my back, I decided to make myself heard until something was done about this oppression. Eventually the driver came back and agreed I could be safely released from what was now nothing less than torture. One hand was freed, but a real flap then ensued when they were unable to take off the other handcuff; various keys were tried, to no avail. Not until we reached Mansfield police station did they manage to get it off. By then my bloodied wrists bore deep grooves and broken skin; I was also having great difficulty in even swallowing my own saliva and suffering from a very bad headache, the results of the chop to my throat and punch to my jaw.

We did not head straight to Mansfield, instead making a detour to the Bilsthorpe Colliery picket where we picked up more prisoners; they also had a large presence that day. When we finally arrived at Mansfield, 'The Black Hole of Notts', we were put into a large holding cell accommodating approximately fifteen men. Many more were in other cells and from what I could see and hear, most seemed to be from the Yorkshire Area – far from home and very worried.

For the uninitiated in these matters it would probably help if I explained the kind of feelings that develop very early in the process. Not being able to see outside time becomes a drag, with even minutes seeming like hours; in all probability one's fellow prisoners are strangers; and the adrenalin triggered by events remains coursing through you, leading to continued anger and frustration. Then eventually a feeling of disorientation descends and you start to ask questions inwardly: what time is it? Does anyone know where I am? Did anyone see what happened?

As far as we strikers were concerned, interrogations inside were regular. Of course, if a man said what the police wanted to hear in interview, things were made easier; if not, their abuse and threats of violence served to heighten the feeling of helplessness. We were told that civil rights were a myth; quite openly they boasted that the only law that existed was whatever they decided it to be. By the end I was convinced that the term 'pitman's language' ought to be 'copper's language', it was so bad.

Of course it is difficult to record close detail of the situation as pens, pencils, paper etc are taken away as a matter of policy along with shoelaces, belts, ties and whatever else you happen to have in your pockets. The mind has enough to cope with without trying to remember much detail: this was not an experience most of us were either prepared for or had tasted previously.

Wednesday 27 June (continued)

The next interview was in the fingerprint room. Again I refused questions and also to be photographed and fingerprinted until I had seen a doctor and solicitor. Here I was told: 'We like fuckers like you. You'll not leave here – only to go to Lincoln.' I again asked for a doctor and was ignored.

At one stage a tall, well-made lad was brought in; he told us he was from Bilsthorpe and had been picked up on his way home from the dinnertime picket. He was obviously a 'ringer'; my own assessment must have been shared by the others as he was also ignored by them. He then just seemed to disappear.

J Strachan was taken out for questioning a second time, but this time he did not come back. I learned later he had been released with a police 'bind over' which meant they wanted rid of someone with the least possible bother to themselves. In effect the acceptance of a 'bind over' was an admission that an offence had been committed without actually saying so.

The numbers in the holding cell were decreasing as the lads were taken away singly for interrogation. I was taken out three times and each one made them angrier than before. The third time however was different: the style and attitude of the officers conducting the questioning was totally at odds with what had gone before. This new approach left us in no doubt that these were men from 'special branch'[6] – the sinister implications were lost on no one. Despite this, I refused to budge from my position and was eventually taken back to the cells.

Wednesday 27 June (continued)

Later I was taken from the cell and into the passage, where two officers attempted to persuade me to comply – they spoke repeatedly of the dire consequences of my persisting. I again asked for a doctor, with the pain in my throat now very severe, and unsurprisingly was told I didn't seem to them to be distressed; at that I walked back into the cell, leaving them standing. A short while later I was taken to what was described as 'an interview with the CID officer'. Again I refused to comply and requested a doctor; back again to the cells with no idea of what I was being charged with, and when. Now alone in the cell, I lay down and prepared to make the best of it. If insisting on what I understood to be my legal rights meant incarceration in Lincoln prison, then so be it. I wouldn't be the first and certainly wouldn't be the last.

> After a time I was placed in a small cell along with a young striker from Shirebrook who had been remanded until the next day. After a while, a sergeant came in and removed the young lad for no obvious reason; when plod came back, he proceeded to read out a list of the charges I was facing from a sheet. To say I was dumbfounded would be an understatement: two charges of assault, one of obstruction and one of ABH, as well as a caution. The door again clanged shut – I was now really alone!

Wednesday 27 June (continued)

Two minutes after he left, a solicitor came finally to see me. She asked questions, filled in an application for legal aid and we immediately went upstairs to the courtroom. Up to now my understanding was that the police would oppose a bail application on my behalf. I was taken into court as one of a batch of nine men; a solicitor immediately pointed out that conditional bail forms were already lying on the table and questioned the legality of the situation. The lady magistrate denied that a decision had already been made and went through the whole charade of refusing unconditional bail in every case. That the whole thing was cut and dried was painfully obvious. My application for legal aid was granted as was an order for my fingerprints and photograph. This was done downstairs – our belongings were then returned and we were taken to the front entrance and allowed out. RELIEF!

> This account of arrest and court proceedings could more or less describe any one of hundreds at Mansfield in those times. Many far more horrifying experiences were had, and the tragedy is that many of them will never be told. Some, however, are very well documented – and should be widely read.

Wednesday 27 June (continued)

Jim Dowen and some of the lads were waiting, having been in court earlier; I was told J Strachan was released at 6.30pm without charge. Good lad! Elsie, I learned on reaching home, had been busy doing her own thing; knowing her as I do, her first reaction on hearing what had happened this afternoon would be shock and fear. She then went along to the pit with I Duncan and there proceeded to roast the superintendent; the 'big 'un', she called him, among other names – much to the delight of the rest of the lads. They then 'stormed' Mansfield police station, which would tell them nothing of me; these ladies are most certainly one of our strongest weapons. As for the Yorkshire lads, after the picket dispersed they were pushed and herded along the road, clear of the village. From there on I have had no report on them. One thing for sure today: the police certainly had their work cut out, containing lads who are totally dedicated to beating the Butcher and his mistress.

Thursday 28 June

A lay-in this morning, feeling rather 'shot at'. I know that my old back troubles are going to start up again. From now on, I'll have to wear both the corset and collar again. The throat and headaches are bad.

I went to the noon picket to find a new mood amongst the lads. They were angry at the police action yesterday. The supt. was looking like thunder; the lads were in great verbal form and he argued about everything.

Due to the number of men now working the night shift, we had to picket tonight. Eighteen men turned up but we only managed to pull one van-load of police, which belonged to the Notts force. The inspector was very touchy and we were lucky not to have some arrested. Approximately thirty-five scabs going in.

Friday 29 June

Slept in again but managed to get down to the centre for just after 6am. One car was sent to Lincoln for the demonstration. The practice of remanding people to prison for charges arising from the dispute has now become commonplace; however, I am not convinced of the use of such demos. More calls to the DHSS: I have to believe that they are part of the harassment, designed to get them back to work. Mansfield was too convenient for us so the operation was moved to Nottingham; claims were then held up because papers were not there – Mansfield had to search etc etc; now Nottingham are managing to lose them as well. It's just not bloody good enough.

Saturday 30 June

Not the brightest of days for me: the week has taken its toll. Took the picket sheets over to Ollerton, where McGinty had a go over the cash we brought back from Pendle – saying if we didn't hand it all over, we might not be paid picket money. I came away resolved that if this were to happen, that would be the day John Lowe ceases to be active.

Monday 2 July

Police this week are from Sussex; their superintendent came out this morning full of smiles. He even shook hands and hoped that we all had a pleasant week, the cheeky bugger. Give me a big picket and I'll chase the smile off his face. Police actions and methods of operation have destroyed my faith, probably for all time, in their impartiality. A call mid-morning surprised me completely: Tim Ormerod and his friends had arrived at the Black Bull, Mansfield Woodhouse, and needed directions from there. B Herbert brought them to the centre: they had brought food and a £300 cheque, which put smiles on our faces. After a cuppa I took them out, determined to get them stopped by a roadblock. Embarrassment for me: never has police activity been so light! Only one roadblock in sight – and that one didn't even challenge. I took them back and let them talk to the lads on the picket line: this time I think they were convinced of the stories told to them!

Flyers tonight for Silverhill: four cars, nineteen men to be there for 5pm. Twilight shift coaling: this is a new switch. At 5.10pm a call from N Duncan: three men lifted, two of them ours – D Lankham and C Hood. Upon their return, the lads' comment was: 'The worst police attitudes we've come across yet.' These Notts bastards are forever looking for trouble: I hope they remember it when this is all over and they are looking to build bridges with us again.

Tuesday 3 July

Midnight shift pickets followed by early days are knackering me. I need to rest, but don't seem to have the chance. Yesterday's events will also take their toll on numbers: with three pickets plus the flyer and the pit gate rota thrown in for good measure, we are asking a lot. These Sussex police are still keeping things low-key, in contrast to our own. Took J Taylor and J Strachan to Ollerton at 10am to act as witnesses for me: the lawyers there took statements from us all. Collected the picket money without the problems I expected: McGinty was not in evidence. Picket payout now goes like a dream: we've organised ourselves such that the whole thing takes little over fifteen minutes.

Picket payout at Clipstone strike centre *(John Lowe)*

Wednesday 4 July

Had a lay-in today, but awakened by 4am nevertheless; what a great feeling, though, to lay back afterwards. Morning was spent letter-writing. GLC told me £200 was again being paid into ladies' account, while a £28 donation from an old people's home also arrived, showing the sort of feeling backing us. Words continue to fail me. My solicitor wants to raise the method used by the police in their application for my fingerprints and photograph in the divisional court in London; this lady is furious at our treatment by both the police and the courts.

Visited the centre at 12.30pm; Sid Walker, it seems, has now decided to visit us for dinner daily. We'll see what happens. A call from a member of the Banner Theatre group in Birmingham who was in the cells in London with M Hood, where she obtained my phone number: she wants to come and spend time with us as we go about our daily business, both in the kitchen and on the picket line.

Thursday 5 July

Morale seems very high on the day shift picket: the lads are doing a limited night picket and still keeping a steady twenty-five on days. A high note when superscab M was cautioned by police for a bald tyre on his car; he was so angry he gave us a double two-finger salute. For this, also, the superintendent is waiting to see him – another caution about his conduct. A cheque from Brighton and one from London today – still it comes in.

A sizeable contingent of Yorkshiremen arrived today; there was no trouble, but the message they brought to the scabs was clear: we'll be coming back when this is all over. These lads then came up for a cup of tea; they wouldn't let the ladies provide food for them, but were delighted at their welcome. The Greek from the Garibaldi chip shop went to the picket line yesterday and stated before witnesses that potatoes he had had stolen from his stock finished up in our centre. I immediately took one lady and one witness to see the Sussex superintendent and reported the matter; he today came to the centre and confirmed that the local police had traced the culprits and the matter was before the courts. I now want a public statement clearing us of this smear. At the request of our colleagues in the North East we have started to compile a list of all our scab neighbours who come from their region; we have also started one for Scotland, Yorkshire and Kent. Blidworth flyers reported a picket of up to 1,000; both the Coal Board and the media are sitting on these facts. Their latest ploy is to arrange interviews for certain of the lads with the colliery manager.

Fifty-one went in tonight, mostly fitters and electricians. This is beginning to alarm me as they seem to be in a position to possibly step up production. The police, I'm told, are now on 24-hour standby. Superintendent D of Sussex: I mark the name because he has been the most humane and understanding one that we have had so far. I still don't trust any of them, but if a man is a bastard, I'll say he is a bastard; if he's a gentleman, then I'll say it just the same.

Friday 6 July

The lads from Thoresby, Mansfield and Bilsthorpe seem to rely on our centre to find out what is happening on a wider basis. No incidents to report but the superintendent called me over when the picket broke up and thanked me for our cooperation during the week.

Cufflinks presented to John Lowe by Sussex supt. *(Jonathan Symcox)*

This puts me in an embarrassing position: if I cooperate, I feel I have failed. This superintendent, however, is a different proposition: he presented me with a pair of cufflinks with the Sussex Constabulary motif on them, with the suggestion that if it embarrassed me, to open the box later. It was pointed out to me later that the thought behind it was a strong point in the defence of the charges against me.

In the 2pm picket managers' meeting the arguments and comments showed a fall in morale throughout the Area, just when our own is picking up. The Burnley trip also resulted in the shit hanging about being thrown at me. I lost my cool: I feel I don't need to prove to anybody my faithfulness to the cause, or defend any actions on behalf of my ladies' group.

Saturday 7 July
H Harpham called for the picket sheets on his way to Ollerton; he also took the scab lists for Scotland, the North East, Yorkshire and Kent. Hope they get them out.

During July, preparations were being made for a family fun day for all our strikers in Nottinghamshire. This was to be held at the Goose Fair Ground in Nottingham which was as central a point as could be found given the problems of the times. Plans had been made by the Sheffield Labour Group and Trades Council and their intention was to send a fleet of double-decker buses complete with food and Yorkshire families to our various strike centres in Notts to pick us up and transport us all to Nottingham. The Cortonwood lads had insisted on two buses complete with food coming to Clipstone; because of the numbers involved, a third bus was allocated to us by the Notts women central committee, making us three double-deckers – but even at that, one would need to make a double trip.

On the day, two of our women went to the junction of the M1 motorway to meet and bring them on to Clipstone. On their arrival at our centre, there wasn't a striker to greet them: as that particular Sunday coincided with our monthly branch meeting, every single one was attending what was for us all a priority and a duty we never missed throughout the dispute. That day we really savaged the opposition due to the local miners welfare day trip falling at the same time; included on the agenda was a vote for the Area Executive, with Clipstone delegate Carrington nominated for a position. Due to the absence of his scab supporters, his efforts came to nought and to rub salt into the wound, he was also mandated from the Clipstone Branch to vote for the new disciplinary Rule 51.[7]

That business over with, it was time to relax on the family fun day: the sun shone throughout, everybody sang and a great time was had by all. Particularly gratifying was the sight of so many of our women and kids enjoying themselves; how they needed such a day – and by God how they deserved it. Although we were a minority in Notts, we were still part of the great majority.

Families travel to Nottingham for family fun day *(John Lowe)*

Monday 9 July

Police this week are from Cheshire and a prickly lot they are. They must feed them well also because they are a real meaty bunch: they look determined to charge straight in, given half a chance.

The Yorkshiremen arrived again at noon: approximately forty from Wheldale Colliery in North Yorks, not enough to cause any real problems for the scabs. We then learned that four had been arrested this morning for refusing to leave Clipstone – again a gross infringement of civil liberties. I took up enquiries on their behalf, finding they were in court at 2.15pm; I informed their centre to find they were still trying to account for a further three. A Snaith called to tell me his case in the High Court in London today for his conditional bail to be lifted was successful. Young D, who was turned out by his parents for refusing to go back to work, today handed over a £10 collection from the Young Socialists. A young lad turned out of his home without food or money – so unselfish when his own need was so desperate. This sort of incident reinforces my faith in ultimate victory.

Tuesday 10 July

Rent-a-mob started off this morning: one ordered two of our lads away from the front of the baths. His reason? 'Because I say so.' I told him what he could do and immediately ordered them back; he backed off on this occasion. Then another incident with a PC at the other end where I was ordered back from the pit gates; I went ahead anyway. I know that I am living dangerously and am being targeted: I shall have to curb my temper because even an obstruction charge could put me in Lincoln at the present time. One of our two cars for the 6am shift at the power stations got through but the other went all over the county, being stopped and warned at various points, before making it there. Yesterday a car-full from Sutton Colliery sent to relieve our lads were arrested at a roadblock for refusing to turn back. One consolation was that the bail was <u>unconditional</u> – we are certainly making progress. After day shift thought I could get an hour's sleep for a change – but was awoken soon after at 7.40am by a call from strike HQ saying they wanted men at Berry Hill at once. An injunction had been granted to get the lads out who sat in yesterday; the police were coming at 8.30am to get them out. Arranged for two cars-full and went back to bed. Two calls again at 8.45am for the same thing: no rest for the wicked.

It seems the lads responded Area-wise and a large force was matched by a very large police presence. Reports said things got nasty for a time; stone-throwing didn't help matters any. I detest the element that do this as it does our cause no good whatsoever; having said that, the continual bullying, abuse, threats, the humiliating way we are herded, the one-sided slant to the media's reporting of the situation plus the courts' handling of it causes the great frustration and anger which manifests itself in this way. An example of the media handling: a Rufford lad last week was sitting at home when a stone was thrown through his window. He opened the door to find a 'working miner' on his doorstep with a bow-saw in his hand. The 'working miner' did such a job that, we are told, <u>130 stitches</u> were needed to repair the damage. He was in custody for forty hours for 'questioning'. If it had been one of our lads, every newspaper and TV station in the land would have made it headline news. As it was, all it warranted was a one-inch mention in the local rag.

Wednesday 11 July

Our branch president is now becoming an old stager as a flyer and seems very keen; I only wish he'd been more committed a few weeks ago. I'm still hoping some gains will be made with him coming over. I had a letter from the solicitor this morning suggesting we may possibly apply for my bail conditions to be lifted. I phoned her to agree and to tell her about the photographs of the arrest. She was immediately pleased at this and warned me to look after the negatives.

On reaching the centre later, it was to find the Yorkshire lads through again in strength; they are making themselves at home and are more than welcome. There must have been over 100 of them today; one car drew up and discharged five passengers – then they opened the boot and two more climbed out! No trouble getting them to the pit, but once there they stood about or sat on the grass and were not as noisy as when our lads are on their own. These North Yorkshire lads don't involve themselves as much as the South Yorkshire ones; they also break earlier, which in turn encourages our lads to do the same. If nothing else, though, it ties up fair numbers of police.

Thursday 12 July

Not feeling on top of the world physically. This makes me angry with myself; when in this condition, I have to rest, but this, in turn, frustrates my belief that leading should be done from the front. John Lowe is not indispensable ... nevertheless, I feel I ought to be there. I had to be at Mansfield Magistrates' Court at 10am – the bloody place was solid! Yorkshire lads awaiting trial along with friends; solicitors and court officials; and what must have amounted to forty to fifty Derbyshire lads and friends. All of these crowded into the courtroom before proceedings started. More by luck than judgement I found my solicitor. At one point the solicitor for the Derby lads took them outside on the pavement to talk, this being the only place available to them. Not a very satisfactory way of conducting what is for us a very serious business. There was no time for my case to be heard today: I now have to be back there at 10am tomorrow.

Jim Dowen phoned later to tell me the £300 we were expecting from National is no longer on. We have £130 this week and the financial situation is becoming difficult again. He did however cheer me somewhat with the news that we now have two branch officials with us: as well as Sid Walker, Jack Fell is joining us from tomorrow. What is happening at Clipstone is the opposite of what is happening Area-wide. We now have to ensure that the bitterness felt by the lads does not turn these people away when they join us; if we are successful, there could be a drift back towards us. I now have a definite feeling that the last big bend has been rounded and we are faced with a long and bitter run-in.

Friday 13 July

Pain in the chest still persisting. The solicitor at court this morning was saying: 'We'll walk all over them.' Problem came later when she was recalled to Ollerton in connection with the thirty-eight arrests at Warsop this morning; I was handed on to a Ms C. She had nine Yorkshire lads who had been in police cells since very early yesterday morning, accused of stealing peas! One spent nineteen hours in custody before being given a conditional discharge – for having 17p worth of peas. The mind boggles at the thought of how this criminalisation of Union members will further develop if or when the latest police bill goes through.[8] As to my own case, Ms C put before the court 'details that were not put' when conditional bail was imposed. The result was an unconditional bail order to appear on 27 July. As my case was the last on the list, I returned too late for the roast pork dinner at the centre – just my luck.

Jim Dowen and H picked us up at 6pm for the social evening in Wellingborough. We had a really enjoyable evening and brought back £150 for the Forum and also a boot-load of food for the strike centre. The ladies have bulk bought this week: half a ton of potatoes, sixty dozen eggs and more stuff from the cash and carry. In excess of ninety food parcels are now needed each week.

> Our women's section was working flat-out: at their peak they were providing 300 dinners daily from Monday to Friday and in addition everyone who was registered with the centre received a very substantial food parcel every week. As well as strikers at Clipstone Colliery, there were also among our number families of men at other pits who lived in the village. Preparations had to begin very early in the day: a prior meeting would have decided what was to be included that week and a visit would then be made to the cash and carry to buy in what was a substantial amount of food. While this was happening, the usual daily routine would be in operation to prepare the midday meal in the centre: there were vegetables to clean and prepare and the kitchen to set out for the lads and their families. All cooking took place on an ordinary four-ring cooker and when everything was on, the heat that was generated was simply tremendous. The inevitable result was that the cooker rings and fittings melted with the heat. Throughout the dispute, two cookers were burned out in this way and a third was only fit for scrap at the end.

Sunday 15 July
A lady has asked to adopt a family for the duration, preferably one with the wife pregnant. D Potter fits this bill nicely and his details were passed on. This is the second adoption we have had: J Strachan and his family were taken on weeks ago by a London family.

Monday 16 July
Ladies' section paid my phone bill this morning so at least our connection with the outside world is maintained; very much appreciated. Without it we were either dead or someone else would have had to take over all the contacts.

Another large Yorkshire presence this afternoon; estimate that it must have been around a 200–250 picket. Not seen so many police in the village for weeks as there are today: two convoys numbering over twenty vehicles and carrying full riot gear. This in addition to all the comings and goings at the pit: a very conservative estimate for this Cheshire lot is about fourteen to fifteen van-loads, again with all the 'equipment'. They trotted out about 140: the bloody road was full of them. At the pit gate a sergeant told me to move to the other side 'or into the van. Take your pick'. I challenged his legal right to do this and pointed out that we were a token picket and not likely to cause any problems but his sarcastic reply was: 'I forgot, Mr Lowe – you only perform for the cameras, don't you.' The bastards glory in such abuse. Bigger and tougher roadblocks at the White Gates and the rat-hole, with our own lads struggling to get through to the pit – S Clayton was held for fifteen minutes. The number of times his car has been checked and details radioed through ... this is just plain harassment. I was even stopped from using the phone today because it meant crossing the road.

Finance was the main item at the afternoon strike committee meeting. With no guaranteed regular payment, we have to be careful, especially considering the number of journeys to power stations/meetings/solicitors etc that must be paid. I suggested cutting the mileage allowance from 9p per mile to 7p – this was turned down.

Tuesday 17 July
A lot of speculation by the lads about the ACAS[9] meeting coming up between the dockers and employers; the hope is that they break down and so keep the pressure up on Maggie. If it stays on for another week, she will be a desperate woman.

Brother-in-law from Markham visited this evening: he has been charged with criminal damage by the Chesterfield police. The alarming aspect about his case is that allegations by three of the four men at work at Markham have identified him as putting down nails welded together; he was at home when picked up then kept in custody for about eight hours. He was released only to be brought back the next day for an identification parade – two men positive, one stating: 'Definitely no.' His experience, knowing him as I do, only proves to me how easily the police can fabricate a case against anyone. This sort of thing can happen to any one of us at any time.

Wednesday 18 July
Slightly better turnout this morning with around twenty-seven men involved. Spirits are very high considering the time of day, the monotony and repetitiveness, the lack of response and the open hostility. The superior officers of this Cheshire lot are intensely disliked, even by their own men.

The talks between the Coal Board and ourselves today went on for much longer than most people expected. The report given by Scargill tonight showed a serious attempt at agreement had been made, with the Board making concessions that surprise me at this stage; however, any settlement must not be seen to be open to claims of a sell-out. After all this time, too many things have happened to us to allow anything short of our just rewards to be accepted. An overriding fear of mine is that there is no concerted lobby from either the Labour or trade union movements against the police bill going through Parliament: when this becomes law, as it certainly will, everything they are at present doing illegally will become legal. Who is to know how far they will then be prepared to go illegally again beyond the new powers? Any future national dispute by whatever union or organisation could be subjected to the blanket and total policing that we have experienced. Freedom of speech, movement and assembly, stop and search, enter and search, strip search, use of the armed forces, fabrication of evidence and collusion with the courts; they will not only be with us, they are already happening. How much more oppression will this <u>lady?</u> be allowed to level at us without a fightback from the wider Labour movement? By the time their heads are out of the sand, it will be too late.

Thursday 19 July
Morning off from the day shift picket; went mid-morning with the intention of facing these North Yorkshire lads and letting them know how I feel about the way they operate: they sit in the centre, drink tea and eat toast, play cards or football, walk around and for the most part don't even try to mix with our lads; they then sit around at the picket contributing little and are first back at the centre for dinner. There was no one in charge of them to speak with, so I took the matter up with a group of them; they were not very chuffed, but I feel both morale and discipline have been seriously undermined this last week. One group yesterday just sat in the centre with no intention of going to the pit until the ladies turfed them out.

Friday 20 July
Having been on a 'bit of a downer' these last two days, I have perhaps recorded comments which on reflection are not entirely fair: the attitude of the lads remains steadfast. The Yorkshire lads started arriving by 7.30am – with just two of us at the centre we were soon boiling water non-stop. With Clipstone seemingly targeted by North Yorkshire recently the only ones to get through are those who come early. With the pit starting half an hour earlier we had to be down at 10.30am; it was a welcome sight to see a 300–400-strong picket in place. In a short time our typical police presence was reinforced by seventeen Transits: the senior inspector nearly did his nut. I was proud of the thirty to forty of our lads who stayed behind after the picket broke to keep the police busy; while ever we stay, they have to remain at their posts. A number of Transits circled the centre after the picket; heaven knows what they expected to happen.

We were sorry to see the settlement with the dockers today. Thatcher has been telling lies all week that their dispute was political and called to aid our cause; this has been shown to not be the case. Their aim in our case is to split the membership from the leadership: their latest ploy is to offer those at work the 5.2 per cent with the promise of back money to 1 November. Sid Walker called the branch committee scabs together to discuss this and surprisingly it was refused by a 7–2 majority. Even so, I hope they are shitting bricks over the new Rule 51.

Sunday 22 July
The campaign by Maggie and the media to cut us off from other sections of the trade union movement could well succeed, so willing is she to buy off support and the media in order to suppress anything in our favour; then there is the character assassination of anyone prominent in the movement. The most disgraceful comment she reserved for herself: when she likened our struggle to the Falklands War, calling us 'the enemy within', her desperation was obvious. Her refusal to accept any responsibility for the state of the economy, blaming instead anyone who happens to be opposed to her, shows the arrogance of her attitude to the working classes of Britain: she is a very dangerous woman and the people of this country will only face up to this fact when it is too late.

I learned today that the lads supposed to go to the power station yesterday did not in fact go. Clipstone falls down!

British Coal had offered a 5.2 per cent wage increase nationally: in doing so, great emphasis was placed on our pathetic financial position. As the annual two-week holiday at Clipstone was due to begin, the extra pressure can be imagined. The difficulty in this period was to find enough activity to maintain the interest of the lads and to continue their entitlement to a payment for picketing duties; the pit picket was an empty exercise with only a skeleton force still at work. We persevered, however, and throughout the fortnight flying pickets went daily to the few pits that were still working. Additionally the power station rota continued so that by the end of the pit holidays most of them had been reasonably well-occupied.

Despite the pit being unproductive for two whole weeks, the police would not take the hint and continued to issue threats against our small picket. They were also giving the lads at the power station hell, confronting them with batons swinging and provocative taunts: imagine the scene, with our maximum four-man picket facing the 'brave blue line'. Their task of making life difficult for the flying pickets was even easier: as 75 per cent of Notts' productive capacity was closed, the number of targets was reduced accordingly and the concentration of police so much greater. This made it more difficult for the flyers to reach any agreed target; in fact we saw an escalation in the number of arrests being made.

One of the many attempts to undermine the activities of the strikers went by the nickname 'Silver Birch'. This was a pathetic traitor who lived in Ollerton and worked at Bevercotes Colliery who said he was taking on the responsibility of talking men in others Areas into returning to work. With the blessing of British Coal and the active support, we were told, of the *Daily Mail*, he was to receive all the attention he was seeking. Unfortunately for our cause he was another who felt no loyalty to his class, a Judas who has only been in the industry for five minutes.

A so-called National Working Miners Committee had come into being and we were told Silver Birch was initially a part of the group. We learnt a great deal of their activities and secret meetings from various sources: the sinister threat of their existence, coupled with the kind of people who were encouraging and helping them, was lost on no one from our side. They would go on to cause us many problems extending well beyond the return to work; the consequences for the National Union would prove very expensive in the long run.

Monday 23 July

Today's monthly Council meeting at Berry Hill did not result in us having access to Area cash. They are also moving somehow to take away our welfare membership, while they intend to seek an injunction against the new disciplinary committee that is going to be elected. These people are injunction-mad – and with Judge M presiding, they'll get it also. They seem, with all their big guns behind them, to be going on the offensive, while we have been caught napping.

Tuesday 24 July

A day shift is just a token picket, with no lorries coming and no pit gate rota.

Numbers keeping up in the afternoon, with some at the pit, two cars at the power station, three at Rufford plus three lads at Sherwood. A picket managers' meeting has been called for tomorrow at 12.30pm – there must be some developments. After some of the rumours we have heard concerning the proposed scab organisation, I hope it's to do with action against them.

Wednesday 25 July

The meeting was made a general meeting at the last minute because Henry Richardson wanted to speak. This was an unfortunate decision – if lads from throughout the Area were not given ample time to get down there for this same chance then it should have remained a picket managers' meeting. Much bitterness was expressed against the scabs and the feeling was that every single one of them has to be expelled from the Union. I tried to make the point that we should concentrate on the shadowy scab leaders with an amnesty offered to the rest, but, although some agreed with me, the suggestion was shouted down. Richardson, for all his sincerity, did not impress me at all: I made the point to him that he should say in the open what he says to us in private and get on the picket line with the lads – not only at the soup kitchens, as he's promised. News of yesterday's Yorkshire effort in blocking the Humber Bridge restored some of the confidence that is ebbing away.

Twelve of us attended the funeral of Paddy McGinley, Ollerton miner, today. Most of the North Notts pits, and representatives of the Yorkshire Area, were present.

Thursday 26 July

Day shift picket gets smaller: anyone would think they had decided to put rest days in themselves. Next Tuesday will be a very small payout. Back at the centre early to find myself lumbered with the spuds: not too bad, really, with the rumbler – it's a great little machine. Food parcels prepared, ninety again. A typical one this week includes potatoes, beans, spaghetti soup, chopped pork, minced beef and onion, meat paste, cream crackers, sugar, tea bags, lard and margarine, cereal and eggs. Occasionally washing powder, tooth-paste, shampoo, soap and toilet roll are included too. This is damn good value, but we must prepare the lads for a reduction in support at any time.

Friday 27 July

My court appearance at Mansfield – I expected to be given a hearing date for Crown Court and, although I wasn't overjoyed by that prospect, I was told I would have a much better chance before a jury. On this I remain sceptical: my faith in British justice is non-existent at this time. As it turned out the police must have thought the same because they dropped the ABH charge, leaving the one of obstruction and two of assault: this way it remains in the magistrates' court. The police practice of dropping charges and substituting others at very short notice means they can play around with countless options they have without any regard for the luckless individual accused, with nobody to challenge them. I am now remanded till 12 October at Mansfield. In the meantime I have to see my solicitor to put my case together.

Arrived home about 2pm from the centre to find the phone ringing: it was a lad calling from the hospital to ask if I could get down there immediately. Our old friend Sid Richmond was in trouble there. What an appalling story! It seems he set out this morning to visit his daughter who lives in Long Eaton; when he reached Annesley Woodhouse he was stopped by police at the traffic lights and told he had to turn back. Being alone in the car and an obvious pensioner, it should have been quite plain he couldn't be a threat to anyone, despite the fact he was wearing our stickers. He insisted he was going forward about his legal business. This was when the police, the London Metropolitan Y Division, became nasty and abusive: they then opened his car door and attempted to pull him out. He resisted and was told: 'Get out, you old bastard,' again and again. His passenger door was opened and five of the big brave Met boys set about dealing with him at once: eyewitnesses, Annesley lads, stated that one of them struck Sid three times in the effort to dislodge him. He was taken to the roadside with handcuffs on one hand and there detained for a time; because he was showing his manacled hand to passing motorists, a constable put his helmet over it and held the arm, hiding it from view. The handcuffs were so tight that the marks were plainly visible late tonight. The rotor arm was removed from his car and when he was allowed finally to go, it was minus his car and with his arm and wrist badly bruised. The Annesley lad took him inside his welfare where he called Sid's son N to come and fetch him. On their way back to Mansfield they were stopped by more police: his son was dragged out of the van, arrested and put in a police van. Sid was taken with them to Mansfield police station, where his request for a doctor was finally granted: he was taken to Mansfield General hospital. It was at this point that I finally had word of what was happening: B Herbert and myself immediately went to the hospital. There we heard Sid's story and, as he was still waiting for treatment, we went to the police station to enquire about his son. They were not very helpful: the young constable dealing with us, who regarded the matter as some sort of private joke, claimed he had no way of finding out about the rotor arm, adding: 'If it's vandalised, he'll have a claim, won't he?' Sarcastic bastards! We contacted the legal centre at Ollerton: their instructions were to say nothing to anyone, and that if anyone contacted Sid for a statement, especially the police, to see them off. They will send someone to see him on Monday afternoon. We rejoined Sid in the x-ray department and from there made our way back towards casualty where a man with 'police' written all over him, behind the softly, softly approach, tried to waylay Sid for a 'chat'. He told us he was from the police complaints department. Sid told him he hadn't yet made a complaint so why was he wanting to chat? He persisted and followed us along the corridor, where he was repeatedly told there would be no interview until a solicitor had been consulted. We saw Sid to his home where we attempted to film his arm. I called the police station on three occasions before I was told, at 5.55pm, that N had been released minutes previously and would be reported for traffic violations. Cynical bastards!

It should be understood that N was in no way connected with the mining industry – his only interest was to see his father receive the medical treatment that his condition warranted. Yet he was dragged from his vehicle and slung into the police van where, with his father unable to assist him, he was verbally and physically threatened; this left marks upon him. After leaving N at the 'nick', Sid was taken to the hospital and callously dumped outside the casualty department by a police crew who didn't care a damn – this a man in his seventies who suffered from thrombosis. I was truly horrified!

After N's release, B Herbert and I went over to Annesley welfare to bring back Sid's car, taking with us a rotor arm. We arrived to find that the police had beaten us to it and put the rotor arm back; likewise they had already taken a statement from one of the three witnesses that we intended to speak to.

Reports of the incident were put out on local radio before they could be doctored; in addition, a camera crew from Central Television who were held up in traffic at Annesley were invited by their lads to film what was happening. Surprisingly, it was shown that same day; but a few days later, when offered a follow-up story, the local radio would not touch us. We were told, by them, that the police had 'leaned' on them and in effect warned them off. We immediately complained to the IBA[10] on the advice of a barrister, but they did not even have the decency to acknowledge it. With hindsight we should not have left the matter there, but such was our workload that I personally had a hundred other matters to deal with which at that time seemed equally important.

Sid Richmond in the company of Arthur Scargill *(Norman Richmond)*

Monday 30 July

Back to the grindstone again; day shifts get harder by the week. I'm afraid that this game is for the young. An industrial cleaning equipment van turned away at the picket: a small success, but a lot of pinpricks hurt. Flyers again to Sherwood Colliery; it seems we are the only pit sending them out during the day. Our own strike committee members are not interested: they either don't turn up or try to take as small a part as possible. They have to realise that responsibility means accepting just that; a testing time for them next week – I think that I'm due a break. Everyone else seems to be getting one but me.

The solicitor who saw Sid today is sure, after going through all the statements, that he has one hell of a case against the police. The advice is to sue for damages against them rather than to prosecute. We have to get maximum coverage out of the story: shit flying the other way will make a nice change. Welsh lads fined £50,000 today after a judgement against them for contempt today; we can expect more of this in the coming weeks.

Tuesday 31 July

I spent a long time this morning phoning Sid's story around: the *Mirror*, *Guardian*, *Morning Star*, *News Line*, *The Miner* and *Yorkshire Miner* are all to call back later. By 12.15pm the *Mirror* had a reporter at the centre looking for a statement. This was given to him, but he obviously still needs to see Sid. I later learned from N that they had managed to contact him at his daughter's.

The *Guardian* phoned later in the day and were given the story by myself. They were very interested, but also need to talk with Sid; they also have to check with the police. Sid phoned to tell me the *Mirror* had contacted him and so we hope to see the story tomorrow. His son phoned me to say that the doctor who saw Sid was so angry that he phoned the local *Chronicle Advertiser*[11] to register a public complaint. The paper phoned N for an interview then me for more background and finally this evening sent a reporter out to Long Eaton to see Sid.[12]

Wednesday 1 August

Bailiffs are due to move in on the Welsh lads today for non-payment of the £50,000 fine. Maggie is easing the way for attacks upon our funds: I expect more injunctions as this realisation dawns on our adversaries. They are now as common as the 'Sun comic'. Shock of the day: cash from National only £2,000 for North and South Notts, meaning only £80 for Clipstone. At this level we will definitely not be able to maintain flying picket support.

Thursday 2 August

What a morning: it absolutely poured down. Eight lads on the picket line and they were worth a bloody medal. Mansfield lads have refused to do the power station any longer: P Deans seems to have lost control of the situation there. If the money dries up, that could happen here.

At afters picket I was hassled by grinning police mouthing barely audible obscenities. I know now I have to keep my head down; I'm not being paranoid about this, as the following explanation will show. Radio Trent have told N that the police leant on them to not follow up the story of his father's ordeal. The IBA also don't want to know. And the further twist: Sid called his son on the telephone from my house on the pretext that his car had broken down and he needed a tow. When his son arrived a short while afterwards, we decided that the call to the IBA should be made from a callbox rather than my house. As they left, I was watching; they were followed slowly by a police Transit which, while they made the call, drove past deliberately, having a good look at them.

At the picket managers' meeting today, it was spelt out in no uncertain manner that we were not honouring the trust placed in us to keep our claims accurate and truthful. Money is very tight on all fronts and prudence is the watchword. I have to plead guilty to this: my practice has been to book any lad taking a holiday so that he may have a payment to come back to. That now has to cease.

Friday 3 August

Sid went over to the legal centre as asked; the old bugger was there all day, finally coming to see me at 5.30pm. They have gone into his case and have decided to go all the way. The writ is being prepared and should be served next week. Now let's see the bastards squirm; I expect a lot of provocation from now on.

Around this time my confidence in our Area strike organisation became very strained. For two weeks running our Area strike meeting had deteriorated into a disorganised shambles with nothing decided or recommended. No discussion of Area strategy had taken place despite our very precarious position. I was also dismayed by an attack on the actions of Ida Hackett of the women's central committee by certain of the Ollerton–Bevercotes delegates present. Ida was a woman of high ideals who, although a pensioner, worked non-stop for us all whenever and wherever she could do some good. That she was active and with us was a tremendous asset to our cause and to hear these comments left a nasty taste in my mouth for quite some time.

At the end of the first week in August, we decided to boost morale with a night out among friends. We left Clipstone in two minibuses, full of enthusiasm, destined for Silverwood miners welfare in South Yorkshire. We had been assured we would be made more than welcome, but on arrival found ourselves shunned while their officials were 'not available' despite the fact that they were drinking only a few yards down the road. Some meat sandwiches had been provided, which proved someone was aware of our visit, but I came away with a greater feeling of isolation than I ever felt back home.

Saturday 4 August

So far in these records I have been reluctant to talk of my own family problems; to keep as accurate an account as possible of my involvement in the dispute, it is right that I should do so. My position is this: my wife is 101 per cent behind my stand. Two sons are scabs, as is a son-in-law at Mansfield Colliery. A row developed in which a daughter-in-law decided that her view was totally right, hence a split. The rest of the family then isolated us both for a while. The result was my wife, always a loving and conscientious mother, teetering

John Lowe (right) with fellow striker Jack Taylor at Silverwood Miners' Welfare *(John Lowe)*

on the verge of a nervous breakdown for weeks; during this time, her only real family contact was with our eldest daughter, who lives in Rotherham. For many weeks she cried herself to sleep nightly, and awoke each morning in the same state. In quiet periods during the day, the same thing occurred: each time was like a knife twisting inside me. The hardest part is not seeing our grandchildren – the worst scenario I could have envisaged, and most definitely heartbreaking. In spite of all this she has remained as strongly behind me as ever; if anything, it has served to make her more determined. Because she knows we are in the right, because she is aware of what is happening, because of the tremendous spirit that has developed between the ladies, she has gradually been able, not to get over, but to rise above the pain.

Sunday 5 August
Friends from Pendle arrived at dinnertime with a boost of food. They've taken two young lads back with them for a week's holiday; unfortunately it has clashed with the Kent and London kids' holidays, otherwise we could have sent four.

Monday 6 August
First day back after the holidays and a twenty-man picket. Surrey police in attendance this week and out in force with us all the time – no problems. Rumours of some of our lads returning this week did not happen.

J Taylor got us all a warning during the afternoon picket by shouting 'scab': the sergeant came forward and threatened to arrest the next one who shouted it. This decision is in direct opposition to the Crown Court ruling the other week which said that there was nothing in law to stop anyone calling out 'scab'. One man went back to work – he's been threatening this for many weeks.

A distressing experience for N Richmond and his wife: have received a love letter from our old friend 'working miner'. Yes, it's the same one – the handwriting is identical – only this time he signs his name 'Ex-deputy, Clipstone'. At some future date I am confident his identity will become known – watch out, pal.

Tuesday 7 August

Cash from National cut yet again: this week it's just £52. The only thing we can do now is stop all flyers: this will barely cover petrol for cars to come to the pit. Just this afternoon we were discussing how to get two of our cars back on the road, with one in need of tax and another of insurance. If the flyers are to be suspended, the lads will have the three-shift pit picket and pit gate rota to make their ten for the week; the main problem with this is one of morale.

Wednesday 8 August

Made the centre with a struggle but had to go back home after the lads arrived. I fell and jarred both my back and neck. On arriving home we found that Pete, our eldest son, has had an accident at work, losing two finger-ends. He has been transferred to Derby infirmary for surgery; this was performed during the night. We then had a lot of trouble trying to locate his wife, who was in Skegness.

Friday 10 August

What a time our kids coming back from London were given: visits to the coast, Houses of Parliament and London Zoo, among many others. Our two lads in Pendle have been equally well looked after: SI, an old ILP[13] member, and his wife had experience of strikes and police actions against them during the decline of the textile industry, but both say the sort of brutality experienced during the present dispute exceeds anything seen back then. The kids from Kent, who stayed in Deal, had a great time too.

Saturday 11 August

The NEC meeting did not give me the boost I was looking for: National need to realise the desperate need at grassroots level in Notts for an offensive. The media battle is wearing down even the staunchest of hearts; for God's sake, Arthur, come to the picket lines and soup kitchens, let the lads and their families talk to you and the rest of the leadership. Listen to their thoughts and needs. Heed their complaints. Help us to take the initiative again.

The ladies, twenty-two of them, travelled to London today for the women's action groups' demonstration. A petition to the Queen was handed in, asking if she could intervene in some way to break the deadlock imposed by Maggie & Co. Some hope!

Clipstone children having fun in Lancashire *(Susan Nike)*

Ladies' section members on their way back from the picket line: Margaret Anderson, Carol Potter, Jane Holness and Elsie Lowe *(John Lowe)*

Monday 13 August

The media still giving mileage to the superscab stories: one-time friend-turned-scab R is doing his version of the Silver Birch, spreading stories about some of the lads returning to work. My interpretation is that he's trying to justify his own actions to himself; hard luck R, you scab. Neil Greatrex[14] of Bentinck is also trying to get in on the act.

Tuesday 14 August

Numbers building – back up to twenty-seven this morning. With the cash cut so drastically by National, even if we had a surge in numbers we couldn't employ them on flyers above the level we are currently operating. Flyers for tomorrow will be grounded.

Wednesday 15 August

The arrest of M Gibson yesterday reached a new low, even by their standards. The lad was wearing a T-shirt lettered as below.

STOP

COME OUT

AND

BACK NUM

SAVE PITS

He has been wearing it now for two weeks without anyone taking exception; suddenly, some idiot takes it into his head to take a scalp. An unpleasant experience for the lad for no reason at all; the police could go into Mansfield and find some really obscene messages printed on shirts which they totally ignore.

Travelled to Edwinstowe for physio treatment with two of our lads who were to go on to Ollerton legal centre. On reaching the Ollerton roundabout, we were stopped and asked the usual questions. We told the truth but were pulled off the road while they 'checked us out'; after fifteen minutes we seemed no nearer to getting through so turned back. We beat them via an alternative route, but the frustrating thing is we have no answers to their bloody arrogance.

By the middle of August our arrest list stood at twelve and a further eight from other pits who had been picked up at Clipstone. This may not seem many when compared with the numbers at many other pits, but it has to be remembered that we are talking of Clipstone and not some place that was able to muster large numbers of men on demand.

Our normal procedure when arrests took place was to first alert our legal centre at the Ollerton miners welfare. If the lad concerned was not local, we endeavoured where possible to contact his own strike centre; we then made arrangements for the lad to be met on his release from custody. If contact with his centre had not been made, Jim Dowen often went instead. We then turned our attention to the search for witnesses; this was not always easy to do at a later date when there had been a large crowd. If any could be identified, they were put in touch with our legal centre for statements to be taken. When cases eventually came to court we were often in a better position to present a case with evidence supplied by eyewitnesses, which in turn presented a solidly-based defence against the usual police fit-up. Significantly, the majority of the Clipstone lads who were arrested were later found not guilty, making the effort well worthwhile.

The local plod in Clipstone differed from his counterpart from away: they practised their own brand on certain individuals in a way that was difficult to prove. For example, towards the end of August one of our lads who lived close by the pit was having trouble at night from certain local youngsters. While the locally-based officer was sat watching in his car, objects were thrown at the house on several occasions. Plod was waiting for the striker to retaliate so he could arrest him, while not once were these young hooligans admonished; in fact they stood leaning on the car of this supposed upholder of law and order while making obscene gestures at the house. If anyone doubts the truth of this story, let me recount the ending of this particular night: our lad had been along the road for a pint at a local pub and was pushing his scooter home when he was jumped on by the police; handcuffs were put in place and he was taken away and had charges laid against him.

Further down the street another striker was also having problems. His car had been tampered with, petrol siphoned from it and he was also subjected to close scrutiny late at night by the same plod. This Little Hitler knew he had a free hand to do whatever he wanted as long as the object of his attentions was on strike. To make complaints against this sort of intimidation was laughable – an empty exercise not worth the time it would waste.

Thursday 16 August

Contacted by Cortonwood strike centre: their lads are walking to Brighton for the TUC conference. On Wednesday night they will be in Clipstone and up to thirty beds are needed. Mick Carter is walking with them; if he manages it, he should be down to a reasonable weight by the time they reach Brighton.

Friday 17 August

Great start today with about thirty ladies joining the picket for the day shift; what a boost they can be. Their comments do get a bit crude at times, but they are straight and to the point.

I arrived at the pit in time for the noon picket to find the chief inspector had been threatening the lads on the gate if they persisted in displaying our 'official picket' sign. On taking the matter up with him, I asked what he would do if I displayed it. His reply was: 'Try it and see.' I then contacted Notts police HQ to complain of his actions and to seek clarification on their attitude. After the usual delaying tactics, I was told someone would see me. It didn't come to that: almost immediately, the lads were told that they could

Official NUM picket sign on display at Clipstone pit *(News Line)*

display the sign. Later on the superintendent came out and passed it off as a mistake. Sometimes we win!

As I am away next week, arrangements made at general meeting. Two new committee members elected, D Carmody and D Broadfoot;[15] J Strachan will look after the picket register, H Harpham to take them in; Jim Dowen will send out the flyers and has current details of problems with DHSS and council rent department in Newark.

Saturday 18 August

Coach for our day out came thirty minutes late; away by 8.30am with everyone in good spirits. We arrived at 11.30am and had coffee and biscuits before we went on to a place in the country called Clarion House – a building owned by the ILP and available to socialist organisations for functions – where they had a ploughman's lunch waiting for us. This was followed by games for the kids; we had eighteen of them with us. The afternoon was an opportunity for our people to get to know these wonderful folk who had given us such tremendous support. Our lads played theirs at football, winning 10–4; parties were taken for tours of the area; Radio Lancashire was in attendance and talked to different men on their personal involvement in the dispute; and a barbeque was later provided which proved a great success. At this point a bag was given to me containing about £50; it was decided we would stay an extra hour to join our hosts for a farewell drink at a local pub – the cash paid for a couple of drinks round the party. We had also been given a cheque for £140 plus £21 handed to us by a lad who had done a sponsored run. With the £5 given by a stranger

John Lowe, in striped shirt, enjoys a pint with fellow strikers and Pendle supporters *(John Lowe)*

on our way there, this totalled a quite substantial contribution. Up to now, I was told, they have put £2,500 forward; it's a sobering thought that without the backing of Pendle, we would have long ago been in serious difficulties as far as our ladies' section is concerned.

Sunday 19 August

Monthly branch meeting 10am this morning; after the last meeting, when we defeated the scabs on every single issue, they really meant business this time. Superscab M was his usual self, on his feet time and again despite the chair ruling about speaking once on any particular subject. We did receive an assurance from the branch officials that 'green labour'[16] would not be employed at Clipstone; this we will have to watch very closely as 'green' recruitment is taking place throughout the Area.

Monday 20 – Thursday 23 August

At last! I'm away from it all for the next few days: we're staying with our eldest daughter in Rotherham. We seem to be glimpsing events from some remote world, as they are shown to and described for most people who are not involved in the dispute. It is sad to think that this rubbish is all they have to base their understanding on; knowing that there is more to it is incredibly frustrating. If only a fraction of the efforts to defeat our strike had been used to try to solve it, we'd have been back to work weeks ago without a lot of the bitterness and ill-feeling that is now going to be left when it's over. The damage to the industry and economy is due solely to Maggie's determination to impose her Tory philosophy, regard-less of the cost.

Friday 24 August
Back home today. Jim Dowen brought me up to date: we lost five back to work on Monday and understandably the lads were upset and downcast. By midweek, however, morale had been boosted again thanks to the visit by the Cortonwood lads and the cock-up by MacGregor[17] in his confrontation with Scargill on TV. Other great news was H Harpham being found not guilty in court and K Butler having his case dismissed.

It seems the media are taking a bit more interest in us: the *Guardian* bloke I chased off the other day did his piece and, I'm told, included the fact that I wouldn't talk to him. The *Daily Mirror* writer Pilger is at Ollerton tomorrow doing an article from our side, I am told again. He's looking for our lads who have suffered intimidation or from acts of vandalism. If this carries on, I'll soon believe that there's a Santa Claus. *Newsnight* are also wanting to film at the soup kitchen; we'll listen to what they have to say. All in all, quite a turn-up. Feeling pretty sick for one of the lads: T Rack having trouble at home and put in a position of having no choice but to return. Anyone knowing the facts would feel for him: he's the only one who's gone back I feel any sympathy for.

Saturday 25 August
Old Sid Richmond came to see me and told me Sid Walker was trying to convince him he should talk to *Newsnight* – and that he'd said they'd been in contact with me. Not true! In any event, his own common sense should have told him the matter was sub judice.[18] I'll make sure he doesn't go through with it.

A Snaith went to Ollerton to speak with *Newsnight*. Some BASTARD has sprayed his car bonnet with the message 'GET BACK TO WORK'. One of these days we'll catch them at their cowardly work; I will approach the colliery to ask for help with the repairs, as they are doing for the scabs. I suppose we know what the answer will be, but as least we can give it a try.

Monday 27 August
No day shift picket on Bank Holiday Monday. Reports indicated that up to 150 men could be working; we had been given to understand that only shaft work would be in progress. Accordingly we checked out the afternoon shift: three workmen and five officials were seen to go in; we were told that only one official was underground this afternoon, with the rest on pit top security patrol. With the police dog patrol as well and aerial surveillance, someone somewhere appears very jumpy.

Tuesday 28 August
I hope I'm wrong, but I have a feeling that we could lose a few more this week. The mental pressure is getting to some: they can see no sign of a fightback. Flyers to Bentinck, four cars, fifteen men; Area-wide we've been running a reduced strategy, with two targets a week dealt with properly.

I later received a call from a lad who was on strike with us for a while to tell me that the overtime ban was being broken at Clipstone – he gave me some names which are to be

Graffiti half cleaned off on bonnet of striker A Snaith's six-month old car *(John Lowe)*

checked out. More importantly he admitted that he was wrong to have gone back and said that a number of the lads were of the same opinion. Asked if he could come to see me, he said he wouldn't mind a chat but was baby-sitting at present. We are to watch out for him and try to set up a meeting with the lads who feel as he does. If this produces a result, what a boost it would be for everyone; especially as he is a fitter – colliery maintenance is stretched and another couple of fitters or electricians on our side would cause serious problems for the pit.

We were hearing stories from inside the pit wall of the recruitment of 'green labour' and the blatant breaking of the National overtime ban to which the Notts Area was still subject. I went to see Sid Walker, who told me 'only miners' sons over eighteen' were being recruited – 'green labour!' Our opinion was that even though he was prepared to scab against us after all – his reasons for returning to work were far from convincing also – his responsibility as a Union official should have prompted him to resist this strike-breaking ploy of the Coal Board.

Later that morning I came into contact with the deputy manager, who had obviously been primed of our interest regarding the overtime situation: he was quite agitated, insisting he had not acted outside any agreement. He had, he said, been in touch with Roy Lynk, general secretary of the Notts Area, and received the necessary dispensation.

At the end of the week, H Harpham and myself paid a visit to the Area offices at Berry Hill to see Ray Chadburn. The overtime incidence, we were told, had been authorised by our branch secretary Alf Hemsley without any reference to our Area officials. As Chadburn was agent responsible for Clipstone, we felt he should at the very least have been aware of what was happening; that he wasn't should have resulted in a bollocking for those concerned. To our dismay, in place of the anger we expected, he virtually gave it his blessing; and as for the 'green labour' problem, his comment was: 'The Board have us by the bollocks.'

Wednesday 29 August
Day shift return with twenty-six on the picket line. Better than I had expected, but a few heads are down at the moment. Christ, Arthur lad, get something moving for them!

Thursday 30 August
Flyers away 10am to Bilsthorpe – four cars, fourteen men. What a report came back from there! As at Hucknall last night, the police were unprepared and we had things our way. When four bus-loads of coppers eventually turned up and disembarked, the lads immediately jumped in their cars and went to Blidworth; on the way they passed another seventeen Transits going to Bilsthorpe! Blidworth was another success and by the time the police got to grips with things there, the picket was over anyhow. Meanwhile, at Clipstone the local fuzz triggered another event: the lads were on the 'green', a little more noisy than usual but in good spirits, when the L Division Met inspector came out and talked with the two locals at the control car. He came across and told the lads to get off the pavement and back on the grass – knowing who had prompted this move, they were upset. After some argument an attempt was made to grab A Gillies; this we foiled by grabbing him back, while H Campbell was also almost taken.

Friday 31 August
A very busy morning today after the picket, spent on the tedious but necessary tasks: long-winded arguments concerning individual social security cases – we lost the one about the special diet, but I had partial success with a special needs payment for a baby born two weeks early – dealing with late benefit payments, school clothing allowance postponed until after the start of the school year etc etc. I then got to Berry Hill to see Chadburn in connection with the 'green labour' problem and the overtime ban.

The afternoon was spent getting everything ready to hand over to Jim Dowen on his return from a break. I can really believe now that my wife and I are going away for a week's holiday. As we have been married for almost thirty-two years and this will be our first holiday on our own, it really is a milestone in our married lives. J Taylor tells us that five babies have been made in the chalet so far this season, but Elsie and I don't give a damn . . .

We remembered rather belatedly that we had not sent a card to our old friend Sid Richmond, who had his hernia operation yesterday. I feel very badly about this as I don't want him to think it's a case of out of sight, out of mind.

Notes
1. Aide to GLC leader Ken Livingstone; later advised Prime Minister Tony Blair
2. General, Municipal, Boilermakers' and Allied Trades Union
3. National Association of Local Government Officers
4. David Gareth Jones died on the picket line at Ollerton on 15 March 1984, just days after the strike began
5. Police mobile detention vehicle
6. Label attached to intelligence units employed to protect the State from subversion
7. Recommending expulsion from the NUM if miners defied National order to strike
8. The Police and Criminal Evidence Act, which came into force on 31 October 1984
9. Advisory, Conciliation and Arbitration Service, a Government-funded, independent body
10. International Bar Association
11. Mansfield and Ashfield Chad
12. Sid's story appeared in several newspapers, local and national
13. Independent Labour Party
14. Founder member and future head of breakaway union the UDM
15. Current Clipstone delegate in Notts NUM
16. People not trained in mining
17. Ian MacGregor, NCB chairman
18. 'Under judgement' – hence inappropriate/an offence to comment on publicly

PART THREE

SEPTEMBER–NOVEMBER 1984

September was now with us and Elsie and I had been offered the opportunity to spend a week at the coast in a chalet owned by Jim and H. Situated at Mablethorpe, it was a facility they had made available to any of our families throughout the summer who could get there: we will always owe a debt of gratitude to them for this. Even though money was in short supply, we had plenty to eat thanks to our support group. We watched a lot of TV, mainly the TUC conference – and although certain people made a lot of comment, we were not fooled for one moment. We had come to realise that both the Labour and trade union leadership tended to be high on rhetoric and very short on substance: unfortunately other people's lack of commitment to us was outside our influence.

On our return, the alarm was set for Monday morning at 3.40am in order to get the flyers away and I was able to resume treatment for my arthritic back: I was visiting the physiotherapy clinic at Edwinstowe which was contributed to by the local pits and staffed by a full-time physiotherapist. At an earlier date, having arrived late for my appointment, I had explained to her that as a striking miner I could not, as a matter of principal, use the free transport provided – driven by a scab as it was. Nevertheless, she proceeded to berate my lack of consideration for her system. When this happened a second time, I pointed out to her that the clinic was not run for her benefit and walked out of the place, never to return. I had been referred there from the Mansfield General hospital and must have been given a black mark, as the specialist seemed to drop me from his appointments thereafter. I relate this story to illustrate the variety and complexity of the problems that many of our people faced: they were not always connected with the dispute itself.

We were entering a new phase of the strike and were seeing the lengths to which the authorities would go to get a handful of men into work. In their efforts to convince the lads that many more were returning after giving up the struggle, they had devised a strategy of loading strangers on to minibuses dressed in wigs and masks so no one could recognise the individuals concerned. A large police presence would be on hand and, at the appointed time, an escort would rush them through the picket. This was happening with increasing frequency in Yorkshire, Derbyshire and particularly along the Notts–Derbyshire border. We had no doubts that some of these pathetic creatures allowed themselves to be used at several different pits but, because of the bizarre circumstances, we could never hope to prove just who they were. Suspicions we had in plenty and we even tried to follow certain ones among them on occasion, but the police net at that time in the morning made the whole operation very dicey. Many people in the future may have trouble believing that such occurrences could make up part of an industrial dispute, but, as laughable as they may sound, I swear that they are the truth.

Saturday 8 September

Report from Jim Dowen showed a very interesting and active week. Two more of our lads were arrested, at Cotgrave, and I later heard that their experience was none too gentle. A Snaith is due in court on Friday. I must organise the people involved in court proceedings to know what is happening and when; our first two were discharged the other week, but things will not happen for us unless we are prepared to work for it.

Jim called me later to tell me of an anonymous donation of £50. This was to be used, the lady said, to 'buy cigarettes and a pint for the lads'. This is a nice gesture as almost all donations are directed to the ladies' section.

Monday 10 September

The flyers had mixed luck this morning at Whitwell. Security was tight but a picket of 600 got through; after a few surges, seven scabs got in – including a couple of the now-familiar 'wigs and masks'.

A lengthy interview tonight, with Jim in attendance, with superintendent G. He is investigating complaints against the police – or so he tells us. He was looking into my complaint about the actions of certain officers on a day last May; I'm not at all certain we should have talked with him, but it was inevitable at some stage.

Tuesday 11 September

Picket payout went as smoothly as normal; I only wish that we could be paying the lads twice as much. I know that the argument is that if they are committed and dedicated, they would picket anyhow, but the £15 penalty on their supplementary benefits is a burden that they should not have to bear.

Wednesday 12 September

Because of a need to organise M Hood's court appearance in London on Friday – transport, bed and sustenance – and the emergence of a new witness for Sid, today looks like being a full day. Accordingly I am leaving the pit to Jim and the lads.

A meeting set up for next week with my solicitor; I now feel a little easier in my mind as at last my defence looks like being discussed. In contrast, A Snaith's defence has apparently not yet been put together and his solicitor has not even been in touch.

Thursday 13 September

Another reasonable turnout for the afternoon picket, but we were not noisy or aggressive enough by half. I suppose that I have to bear the blame for this: if I wasn't involved in so many aspects of the whole thing, I would at least be able to pay more attention to keeping them on their toes. At the meeting after dinner a lot of bitter comment came out on this matter: generally the feeling was that yes, we need to waken up our ideas a bit, but no, they won't get involved in violence unless they absolutely have to. Also, after an incident at the Mansfield flyer last night, they agreed they would try to snatch back lads who had been lifted – but only if we match the police for numbers.

A call later from London to say that M Hood's case has been dismissed. Fantastic: we now stand 3–0.

Friday 14 September

Five cars of flyers, eighteen men, away by 4.30am to Bevercotes – they have their re-ballot after the police refused access to the lads on strike first time around. During the early hours, so the news tells us, 2,000 pickets were turned back; four of our five cars got through after doing a lot of mileage. I am now convinced that our strategy is too predictable: if lads had been directed to hit two different targets, we would have achieved a much better result. The police again prevented the lads from voting.

Our own picket of twelve men has made the first full count in weeks. The result surprised me: for the three-shift 24-hour period, there were approx 900; this is showing well over 400 men still away from work. Allowing for sick notes and rest days, we must have well over 100 on strike. The attitude of the men has changed greatly today: they are more verbally aggressive than in a long time and the scabs are hearing more truths about themselves than of late. This afternoon a Canadian camera crew showed up – the first in a while I haven't told to piss off.

Ian MacGregor *(News Line)*

News that the talks had broken down came as no surprise to me but I know that a lot of our people were dismayed when they heard it. It has been obvious from Leon Brittan's[1] disgraceful comments on 'life sentences for picket line jack-boot thugs' that any settlement chance would be sunk before it got too far. Maggie's puppet MacGregor has no authority to negotiate independently to end the dispute and now they barely bother to conceal the fact. I'm afraid that this is now a 'fight to the death'.

Despite this knowledge, our people still prayed for a settlement with honour. They were magnificent, loyal to the cause and brave beyond question – but they were also human. In the privacy of their minds, they feared what the future would hold if the fight was lost with the cruelly vindictive likes of Margaret Thatcher, Leon Brittan and Peter Walker[2] continually putting the boot in.

The dispute had developed into a cat-and-mouse chase with the police. After all that time, any dialogue with those going into work had become impossible: they simply refused to discuss the issues with us. But if some sort of discussion somehow had taken place by the roadside, the police would have dropped like a ton of bricks in order to keep the divisions alive. The daily routine therefore developed into a charade where the scabs tried to pretend we were not there while the strikers tried to make them feel as uncomfortable as possible. And the attitude of the police had to be seen to be believed: the Notts force, as well as threatening our lads, were telling them: 'You should be inside and working. The strike is unconstitutional and you strikers don't even know what you are striking for.' Our targeting of other pits had also become directed at outwitting the police as much as causing discomfort to those working.

Also during September, tonnage figures were circulated: we at the Clipstone pit were having a far greater effect on production there than was the case at many of the Notts pits. A comparison of tonnages for the weeks ending 29 October 1983 and 27 September 1984 showed that production was down by 59 per cent, from 20,526 to 8,400 tonnes. If that kind of result had been general throughout the coalfield, a totally different result to the dispute would, I am sure, have been seen. For the week in question, only Linby Colliery had better figures, showing a reduction of over 62 per cent.

Saturday 15 September

Down at the centre by 7.30am to get ready for the trip to Barnsley today. The speeches from Jack Taylor,[3] the NUPE lad and Arthur were great, but I'm afraid Wedgie Benn did nothing to move me this time. Afterwards we went with the Dodworth lads to a pub in Barnsley and finished the afternoon with a really good sing-song. It wasn't the most uplifting of days, but just to see the lads' pride in at last walking behind their own banner made up for some of the many disappointments of late.

Sunday 16 September

Today was our granddaughter's second birthday and her party was held at our house. The first family get-together since the dispute started; with one exception, we were together again.

Monday 17 September

Mid-morning I contacted Dennis Skinner, Labour MP and childhood acquaintance, on behalf of our Pendle friends: they are wanting someone to speak up there and would love it to be him. Dennis is speaking in Accrington during Blackpool conference week so there is an opportunity to get him to Pendle; he is willing to do this, if it can be arranged. We found out this morning that a wheel is missing from the banner. We had been told to keep it in the strike centre before transferring it to the miners' welfare this morning. During the weekend the cadets have had use of the St John's hut; it seems to me that someone is trying to discredit us, as we know that it was returned from Barnsley intact.

Tuesday 18 September
Flyers today to Annesley. First reports show a very interesting afternoon: the 250 assembled had taken the police by surprise. When they brought their reinforcements, the lads moved on to Bentinck; here again they were caught completely on the hop. Young A Snaith was followed and threatened with a beating and having his car turned over. From there the lads again moved, this time to Hucknall; again the police could do nothing but follow on later. They were from the London Met and said to be very angry. Sadly, we are restricted to this kind of action instead of debating the real issues; we are making no impression on the 'Notts mentality'.

Wednesday 19 September
This morning the Essex police tried to stop the lads from shouting; they say complaints have been received from people nearby. They also tried to take the official picket sign away; the superintendent later apologised for this and tried to show his impartiality by giving instructions to his men to act against the scabs also when the occasion demands. No wonder we get confused.

Went through to see my solicitor this afternoon with my two witnesses from Dodworth; after a lengthy discussion, discrepancies in the police statements showed which gave rise to hope for my defence. If they stick to their stories we have a great chance as there are so many lies in what they say.

Thursday 20 September
Flyers away by 3.30am to Kiveton Park Colliery – three cars, ten men. By the time they left, I was so knackered I could have slept for a week; I've got a dose of flu coming on. Returned to bed but was knocked up to be told five of our lads had been arrested and taken to Chesterfield police station. With five in jail and a car out in the wilds, I had to get over there.

They were stopped at a roadblock just before they left the Yorkshire border; strange because they were not outsiders trying to get into Notts, but Notts lads trying to return home. Because they refused to turn around, they were set upon by the police. J Brown was dragged from his car by his head which was then banged into the side of the police van – he was told he would 'be done' for damaging police property. A Cornell was followed as he ran from his car, grabbed and taken between the vehicles and punched repeatedly. Attention was then turned to the cars themselves: the first was pushed off the road into a ditch and an attempt was made to do the same with the second, but the steering lock was on and the wheel was turned the wrong way. When they were finally seen to in court, I was disgusted: total bail restrictions until 15 and 16 January 1985. In effect this takes three cars off the road and five men off the picket line – a real body blow to our strike branch.

Police roadblocks, a common sight during the strike *(News Line)*

Our hope for the immediate future is that the deputies[4] will come out and vote to strike. Although theirs is a different issue, the added muscle can only boost the lads. Fingers crossed! My fear is that, even if they vote to strike, Butcher MacGregor will buy them off. Even though they do not vote until next week, we are told that he has already arranged to meet their leaders for talks on the issues involved.

Friday 21 September
After court yesterday we now have a pool of lads who require activities to keep them busy; they can start by cleaning out the centre and tidying and stacking the food. After that, besides manning the kitchen for the day shift, other jobs need to be found, such as logging and helping others who have jobs that need doing.

I arrived home to begin packing a bag for the Labour weekend school in Whitby. The nine of us finally got away by 4.30pm, arriving there at 7.10pm; I'd forgotten the programme and didn't know where to head for. Eventually we arrived at the Metropole just in time for the evening session, a talk by former Yorkshire Area Executive member David Douglass on 'The miners and the media'; this was an impressive performance. A lively discussion followed, while some videos were also shown. These tapes are very important as a morale-booster; although we have two, we have not, as yet, made use of them.

Saturday 22 September
Very good morning session with Roland Boyes, MP for Houghton and Washington, as the speaker; the subject, 'Unions and the media 1984', is very relevant at this time. I hope some

of those present did not resent the extent to which our dispute took over the session. The afternoon was not quite so interesting: the style of speaker Regan Scott, national secretary of the TGWU, was clinical and delivered as if intended for someone else instead of John Lowe and friends. Although he had a microphone, he didn't use it; his audience, therefore, were straining to hear what he had to say throughout.

The night was devoted to a social get-together, a huge success. The Whitby Labour section had certainly gone to some lengths to ensure a good weekend for everyone: paying our expenses, waiving our fees and putting us up. What really strikes me is the difference in attitudes of the Labour people in constituencies held by the Tory Party and those in our own miserable area.

Sunday 23 September

We were on the road by 7.15am in order to be back in Clipstone in time for the branch meeting. What really set the seal on things for me there was when the secretary read out a letter from, of all people, Her Highness the Iron Lady Thatcher: this was to congratulate the Clipstone scabs on the magnificent fight that they are putting up. What next? The bastards also rescinded a minute from a previous meeting when we had managed to vote for the new Rule 51 – one man, M, is succeeding in running meetings from the floor at present.

Monday 24 September

A real cock-up – I slept in and the lads had no bread. I deserved the comments that I later received. Mrs B from the legal centre called to deliver her usual bag of potatoes – another lady whose support has been constant throughout. She was telling me of the uncertainty of the future of our legal facility there. In better news, Berry Hill agreed to pay for us to replace J Stone's broken windows. With him just coming out of hospital and having young people in the house, I am relieved.

A very serious situation arose when the existence of our legal centre was threatened. The centre was staffed on a voluntary basis by lawyers who were members of the Haldane Society of Socialist Lawyers: they had come into the county to handle our interests on all matters related to the mining dispute and were generously and commendably giving of their time. Our need of them was growing – had we lost their assistance, our plight in the courtrooms of Nottinghamshire would indeed have been fraught with danger. The problem, we were told, arose when Hopkins & Sons had complained to the Law Society about the actions of our lawyers who, they were claiming, had no right to be operating thus. The situation was to cause us some anxiety until it had been resolved in our favour. If the Law Society had upheld the claim, we could have found ourselves in serious trouble.

Around this time we received a report from the Haldane Society concerning their investigations into the policing of the dispute to date. They had extreme reservations about the methods being employed by the police against strikers and the blatant disregard for accepted normal court procedures, particularly in magistrates' courts;

another very unsettling aspect was the wide disparity in the sentencing that was being handed out by magistrates in different parts of the country for similar types of charges. Common sense would suggest that it should not only be those on strike alarmed by such a situation; I suppose choosing to pass by on the other side can become a way of life.

Tuesday 25 September

Fair turnout of twenty-two lads; by 5.45am the noise of their shouting had once again brought threats from the police 'brass'. I asked the lads to give the scabs more verbal; armed with taunts of Maggie's letter, they responded and some of the scabs were absolutely bloody hopping – they didn't like it one little bit. The picket payout was cocked up by Jim Dowen not having the book prepared; I know that he has a lot on his plate, but J Strachan had prepared the payout list for him. The result was a chaotic fifteen minutes with John Lowe at the centre of an irate crowd.

Only one car, four men away flying tonight to Ollerton; I was expecting them to have a hard time getting there, but their report shows a different story. There was a large police presence to control a modest picket; when the 'meat wagon' was brought in it provoked some protest which resulted in a police charge. In the confusion, police charged into the nearby pub; the lads said that they had never seen a pub empty so fast. Nine arrests followed all this, but the most disturbing aspect was that, after it was all over, more than a hundred were cordoned off and kept there for one and a half hours.

Wednesday 26 September

Our five 'pensioners' prepared bacon and eggs this morning, which went down very well; their morale is reasonably high at present, but we'll have to watch it. Later they fetched the glass and repaired J's window – I'm told they made a very good job of it.

F Childs,[5] manning our new token picket at the plant pool, threatened with arrest. We approached this sergeant and were referred to the inspector; he agreed to accompany us on a walk around the area. On this we tried to make him see reason, but he was adamant that we were not allowed to place a picket there because if another person arrived and attacked the picket, it was he who, purely by being there, presented the threat to law and order. In short, the most illogical load of shit I've ever heard; as F put it later, it was like blaming the victim for the crime.

Thursday 27 September

Polish reporter 'The Miner' told me about yesterday phoned asking to be picked up and a car was sent to Mansfield. After a lengthy chat he expressed a wish to talk to the scabs; I told him he wouldn't get any help from me. This ploy was unsuccessful as his English was adequate enough to see him through. He also talked to the ladies during the dinner operation and food parcel distribution; he was impressed by their energy and determination.

The NACODS ballot is causing quite a lot of speculation. A big majority for strike is forecast; early returns would suggest this. However, I expect them to settle and keep working. If this was seen to go wrong for us, I expect to lose a few more lads; although I would be disappointed, I don't think, in all honesty, that I could blame them. Hang in there, lads!

Friday 28 September

Two of our lads and two from Mansfield Colliery are painting a pensioner's bungalow and greenhouse this week; I don't mind them being away from the picket line on these sorts of jobs as we see it as a PR exercise. The five grounded ones are also doing a great job at the centre: in all its years, it can never have been cleaned so much. We learned today that we are expecting another 'strike baby'; we've already had two and this one only has a few weeks to go. Why the lad didn't tell us, I can't imagine. He should have been getting help from the ladies' section before now; we'll see him all right.

A Midland spokesman for the deputies is saying that there'll be no strike. Apparently NACODS wanted the Bishop of Durham [David Jenkins] at their meeting after his comments the other day seemed to put God on the side of the NUM – they have to have the same, plus 10 per cent. Clipstone NACODS today was moved to donate £1,000 to our ladies – only six voted for this. We'll remember when the time comes, as it certainly will. Meanwhile the scabs have met the Board to ensure payment in the event of a deputies' strike: they were told that they must report for work, but that no commitment can be made over wages – poetic justice for their treachery to the Union.

Monday 1 October

The two Manton scabs who brought the injunction last week were due to report for work today; it wasn't difficult therefore to guess what would happen this morning. Actually the games started last night – the whole area was sealed off almost the entire night. Clipstone didn't send anyone, as it wasn't designated an Area hit; lads from Ollerton and Mansfield then turned up at our pit, having been on the road since 3.30am. An alternative target could have been set simply because the police were expected to be out in force.

The Post Office van driver today went through our picket line without giving the lads a chance to talk to him; he was very upset when I took his number on the way out. The Labour Party conference started today, with Scargill receiving a standing ovation before he spoke then a two-minute one afterwards. Yes, he spoke well enough and the vocal support was there – but oh for some bloody muscle!

Mansfield lad K Wyville has still not lodged an appeal. His case was brought to me today and what I learned appalled me. He hasn't changed solicitor from 'H the Hopeless' and was completely demoralised, being in his cell for 23 hours a day. I arranged for his wife to be contacted with a view to seeing solicitors at the legal centre.

> Wyville had been sentenced to nine months' imprisonment in Lincoln for allegedly striking a working miner. He was one of our own, catered for by our women's support group. From what we knew of the case, it was a complete fit-up with the police concerned only with matching a scalp to the complaint. No one disputed a punch

was thrown but, we were assured, the police knew that K was not the one who had thrown it when they decided to proceed with their charges. As far as they were concerned, the fact that he was a striker was justification enough. A subsequent appeal failed and the lad had to do his time. Needless to say, he lost his job.

The day-to-day business of the group carried on seemingly without discord, but it would be stretching credulity to expect the reader to believe that arguments did not develop at times. One such incident at the strike centre saw Jim Dowen and myself on one side and some of the women's group on the other. I had asked one of them to discuss with her committee our need for help in funding a car insurance; up to that point, we had paid from our own strike fund – without asking for help – seven full car taxations, one half-paid, £20 towards an insurance and numerous payments for cases of hardship. We felt we had done a very good job keeping our cars on the road. Not unreasonably, therefore, we felt that as the cars were also available to the women's group, some help would not be out of order; the response was that it was the responsibility of 'Ollerton'. By this they meant that we should be asking the Area strike fund for whatever assistance we needed. We were also accused of discriminating against those cars where the driver was 'grounded'. Given our situation, these sorts of comments were not very helpful – and were, in fact, hurtful.

As transport costs were a problem common to all groups, it was realised that some action had to be taken locally to alleviate the strain on our resources: we were given permission to make street collections in Nottingham on a strict rota basis. Each branch was allocated their collection dates with the instruction that no more than two men would be operating at any one time. Our first effort for Clipstone on Friday 5 October was to realise the sum of £82; even though it was not our biggest collection, it represented a vital injection of lifeblood into our finances. Although the collection was now a priority, it added to our already-overloaded list of commitments.

The sickest story of the whole affair unfolded when a letter was sent to the parents of David Jones, the young man who lost his life on the picket line at Ollerton Colliery at the beginning of the dispute. It was printed on paper bearing the headline 'National Working Miners' Committee' and, expressing the deepest sympathy from this bastard organisation, had with it a cheque for £250. The outrage felt by Mr and Mrs Jones, mirrored throughout the coalfields, was expressed plainly in their reply, while they tore up the cheque.

Tuesday 2 October

The police have been threatening to arrest again for shouting; the trouble always starts with the local snakes in the control car insisting that their ideas of control be observed. I've not heard of any other picket line being threatened to this extent. Some of the scabs are distinctly uncomfortable when going through while a lot more are now being openly abusive. The two in court at Bingham have not only had their bail conditions lifted, but their application for legal aid granted; how can such variations in justice exist? Courts such as Mansfield and Chesterfield must surely one day be called to account for the judgements they are delivering.

Further talks today between the Board and NACODS: NACODS are suggesting joint talks between BACM,[6] NUM, the Board and themselves. Our leadership today served with a writ inside the conference hall; their reaction, predictably, is to ignore it. They will now be either jailed for contempt or fined; when the fine is then ignored, sequestration of National funds will take place. All part of the 'great plan' – the two Manton BASTARDS who have fronted the situation have something to answer for. The Notts scabs have, by inviting the lawyers and judges into our rule book, started a chain of events that will outstrip Spencerism. The potential for disaster for the whole working class is now great that the civil unrest the police are now trained for surely cannot be avoided unless the catalogue of anti-union legislation and the police powers laws are repealed. How we need a Labour Government at this time!

Wednesday 3 October
A cheque from Pendle this afternoon; called them this evening and they say another, a collection taken during the Dennis Skinner meeting, would be arriving this week.

Thursday 4 October
I only just made it to the picket line this morning; I am worried by the subdued atmosphere I found amongst the lads. Afterwards I made my way back home to bed. So much to do, and I can't do anything about it.

Friday 5 October
The Labour conference ended with everyone hailing it a success and confident they were on their way to an election victory. I'm afraid that they still have to arouse an apathetic electorate then convince them; media bias has to be overcome before any effective message can be put over. Talks today between the Board and NACODS ended without any agreement. They are meeting again on Sunday. It was reported that if no agreement was then reached their members would be called out.

Sunday 7 October
An alarming development in the case of Sid Richmond and his son: the police visited N yesterday and asked questions regarding the case against the police. Bearing in mind the writs served against them, it seems a very questionable tactic on their part.[7]

Talks today between the Board and NACODS resulted in no agreement. They are now asking for talks with ACAS: we could be forgiven for thinking that they are afraid to call a strike in case it is construed as being in support of the NUM. For all the heat and noise that was generated at the Brighton TUC, I now have a feeling of isolation greater than at any time during this whole affair. As far as the authorities are concerned, we are the new Jews; as far as our trade union comrades are concerned, they'll throw their few bob in the tin and that's their bit. Maggie will still keep us isolated because no one wants to be seen physically to be helping us. Where do we go from here?

Pendle Constituency

Labour Party

27 Every Street,
Nelson,
Lancs.
Tel. Nelson 62573

1·10·84.

Dear Elsie · John,

Just got home from the Denis Skinner meeting. A lively meeting as you can well imagine. We raised £75 collection plus a cheque for £60 which I've sent to you right away.

I think someone is coming down at the weekend but Stuart will be getting in touch with you later in the week.

Malc sends his regards & says to tell you he still uses Sweekex.

Best wishes.
Anne Malc · Nick.

Letter sent to John Lowe by Pendle supporters *(John Lowe)*

Monday 8 October

It's beginning to dawn on me that my day of reckoning comes on Friday. I expect the worst, bearing in mind the hostility from some of the locals. Notable amongst these, of course, is PC 'Faint-a-lot'. As he is one of the witnesses against me, I expect him to try to swear my life away.

Afternoon picket poorly attended, with no more than twenty-five bothering to turn out; if we were sending flyers at present there'd be no bugger at the pit. The scabs will still not face us as they go through. Although we're not giving them much verbal at present, they don't like being stared at. My contempt for them knows no bounds. I'll be out in the morning looking for my youngest son; although it's like a knife in my chest when I see him pass us, that's nothing to what he's doing to his mother.

Talks today between NACODS, NCB and NUM will be going now to ACAS on Thursday. I'm not happy about a third party being involved in our talks on pit closures, which is what NACODS are pushing for at the present time. If they had any backbone at all, they would be bringing things to a head by joining us: when the Board start on a closure programme, any of their members who cannot be absorbed will be subject to re-grading instead of redundancy. Thatcher is taking some stick at present, at least more than she's used to; she's had the Bishop of Durham criticise her, now the Archbishop of Canterbury and the Bow Group[8] of her own party. I don't doubt, though, that she'll get them back into line in time for their circus at Brighton.

Tuesday 9 October

Essex police out and in position very early. Each new lot we have now come out as if they've been instructed to keep their distance; I suspect we are now regarded as hostile. Hope it stays that way.

Flexing their muscle this afternoon, saying no children would be allowed on the 'green' and to take them away. They were told that if they did anything about it, a thousand including kids would be here tomorrow.

Flyers tonight at Rufford – reports say the police were outnumbered for once until the Notts mob came on the scene. Immediately they charged and scattered the lads; the picket had begun to disperse when they cut loose, with chaos resulting as the lads tried to get out of the way. Two arrests were made, one being A Ashford, one of ours: he's in the cells until tomorrow.

Wednesday 10 October

Interesting turn at the afternoon shift picket: following our shouts at the scabs, the police came on to the 'green' and encircled us – they were like dogs straining on the leash. The lads proceeded to take the mick for the rest of the picket and stayed an extra twenty minutes to keep them from their rest room.

It was 4.30pm before the lads arrested last night were in court. The usual Mansfield charade was played out, with bail restrictions imposed and legal aid refused. Minds are made up before we go in; our situation is hopeless. The legal centre is not staffed very well with solicitors this week: unable to accommodate Sid and son regarding the police harassment of late – the first time I've been unable to get statements taken in months.

Thursday 11 October

Kitchen duties once again this morning – I don't think the lads appreciated the rubber eggs that we served up. I have to admit that John Lowe is not exactly the best cook in the world.

One of our lads has been taking his dog with him of late and was on the 10am–12pm stint on the pit gates. Nothing was said to him for the first hour, until we had established the picket; then the inspector came out and ordered him to get away from the pit. The lad complained to me and I told him to put the dog on the 'green' and no more. The inspector didn't challenge but I let my feelings get the better of me and chewed at two or three of the lads for talking to the police. Neither side liked what I said, but it was effective.

Friday 12 October 1984 was crunch day for me: the moment of truth had arrived and I fully expected to be on my way to Lincoln with a custodial sentence by the time it was over. We arrived at the Mansfield courthouse at around 9.40am and after some discussion with my lawyer, we were in court by 10am. This was the start of a diabolical sequence of events; an utter miscarriage of justice.

The first police witness was the Clipstone-based officer from the Notts police whom the lads had christened 'Faint-a-lot' because of his seemingly nervous disposition. His account of the event of the day in question was so far from the truth as to be in the realms of fantasy. Bearing in mind he was answering questions under oath, his story was entirely different, not only to our version of events, but from that of his colleague who was a member of the Somerset and Avon force. He stated that I threw a punch with such force that his attempt to intercept it caused him to over-balance. The impact was such that although he still maintained his hold on me, he went down, pulling me with him to the ground. Incredibly, the same punch also caused his colleague to lose his footing and he fell with us to the ground. At that point I was alleged to have started to throw more punches that resulted in his mouth being cut while at the same time kicking out and injuring his colleague. What a start he made to the case for the prosecution.

He then changed his story to say that rather than my hitting him in the mouth, he now thought that when we fell to the ground my head hit his face and that was when his mouth was cut. Considering he had had two or three months to think of what took place, the magistrate's acceptance of this disturbed me. The truth was that at no time till we were actually on the floor did he touch me: the two officers who grounded me were not even in court.

He went on to say that I had been pulled to my feet on two occasions before being handcuffed. This was a blatant falsehood as I was on the ground when the handcuffs were applied, verified later by his own colleague. His fairytale continued with the assertion that I was 'dragged' – emphasised – to the mobile cell block by two other officers. These were all definite points, stated quite openly by him.

The second police witness put under oath denied right away that he was pulled to the ground. His version was that he knelt down on one knee to 'assist' in what was taking place. He made no allegation of any punches being thrown, although he did say that I kicked him. Quite where he did not explain to the court and his vague allegation was never questioned by the Bench. He said I was wearing heavy industrial boots and this we challenged as my pit boots were still in my locker in the pit head baths. He then changed his description to 'heavy industrial-type shoes'. When challenged yet again, he changed his mind once more to describe them as 'heavy shoes'. His version of the actual arrest was a little more accurate than that of his co-witness.

Because of the widely differing accounts they had given and the fact they were changing their stories as they went along, we approached the Bench and invited them to throw out the charges against me. They decided to adjourn in order, they said, to deliberate; on their return, we were dumbfounded when they ordered the case to proceed – and from that point on it was downhill all the way.

The prosecutor grilled me and his sarcasm at times brought protests from my solicitor but no admonishment from the Bench: he was telling me that I was lying and that the whole affair was put on for the camera. My two witnesses were accused of lying and one was told by the prosecutor that he was not even present at the scene, despite the fact that he was arrested shortly after myself only ten yards from the spot where I had been lifted.

Friday 12 October

Given the testimonies we had heard, I was stunned by the verdict: guilty of obstruction, which I expected, not guilty of the first assault, guilty of the second assault; £75 for the obstruction, £125 for the assault, court costs and witnesses' expenses of £164. A total of £364 for sitting on the bloody grass; they saved their consciences by freezing it until fourteen days after the end of the strike, then to pay at £10 per week. What this fiasco serves to prove is that we are guilty even before we walk into court. Their determination

Arrest of J Strachan outside pit walls *(John Lowe)*

to set an example was further highlighted by the clerk of the court pointing out on two separate occasions that the court costs of £132 could be paid out of public funds. To say that we are pig-sick would be to greatly understate our feelings: we are all bloody disgusted with 'British justice'. The question of an appeal now rests with the solicitors; we have been told that all fines over £100 would be contested anyhow. On reaching home around 5pm, the phone was continually ringing from friends anxious to know what had happened: this, at least, helped to restore some of my faith in human nature. We have been lucky up to now, with four bail restrictions lifted and three who have won their case; today changed all that. I don't like to think what the courts are going to do with the others coming up: we still have another twelve not counting the three who are now scabbing.

The talks at ACAS have been adjourned until Monday. MacGregor is making noises to suggest that our leaders are prepared to compromise. If anything of that nature happens, I'm afraid that they might as well resign. We've lost and suffered too much already!

Saturday 13 October
After getting quietly drunk last night, a very quiet day today with no contact with anyone.

Sunday 14 October
This afternoon it was good to see our old friend SI with his party down from Pendle. They brought clothing and footwear, food and a cheque for £200. They seemed to enjoy their stay and the opportunity to engage in argument? discussion? with the local church was a highlight. Concannon MP[9] had been to church and with the rest of the congregation had visited the senior citizens centre next door. We took the chance to let them know how we felt about a number of matters: as usual Concannon would not involve himself in such things – the eternal fence-sitter.

Monday 15 October
Story this morning that J had been in the cells all night. An argument developed between J's family and a number of nearby families which resulted in his daughter being assaulted by the scab next door; when J went to her assistance, he was in turn set about. Their bodies and faces bear testament to this today. As is to be expected, only J, his son and a teenager from close by were arrested; none of the scabs were touched. Two vans of police, Panda cars and a dog vehicle were brought in. When they got them to the cells, J apparently caused them a few problems by being uncooperative – they were pleased to see the bloody back of him. He wouldn't sign a bail form; the lads were let out much earlier, having signed. I've advised him to get himself and his daughter examined by a doctor tomorrow, while I'll obtain a Polaroid camera from somewhere and take pictures of their injuries in case further charges of assault are forthcoming against J. He's also to see the solicitor when we go to Ollerton for the picket money.[10]

Tuesday 16 October
One game these Dorset lads play is to fix you with a stare individually and see how long you will stare back; I find I can hold my own at this intimidation game without any trouble.

A food delivery from France – it was quite a job deciding what the individual labels meant. Starting at about 2.30pm, it was 8pm before everything was recorded and stacked away. What a satisfactory job. This is the first one that we have had from the continent; hopefully it will not be the last.

An alarming story: the Creswell food kitchen was burned down yesterday. It seems arson is claimed by the strikers while the police just don't seem interested. It took them forty-five minutes to get there, while a scab complaining can get them out in minutes. Later reports said that chairs, paper and tablecloths were piled in the centre and fired; entry had been gained by breaking a window. Only the bravery of one of their ladies, who rushed inside and turned off the gas heating which was due to come on, prevented a disaster. As it was, the downstairs area was gutted. The scab workers committee had been holding one of their traitorous meetings the night before … coincidence?

Wednesday 17 October
Took up J Strachan's application for coal due to the illness of his son; his doctor wouldn't write a certificate for him, saying he would phone instead. On seeing the manager Mr Daniels we found he had received no call, but he said that if one was made, the coal would certainly be forwarded. He's been a gentleman so far – I believe him when he tells us something.

An announcement by NACODS that they would strike from next Thursday has certainly put the cat among the pigeons. If certain deputies decide to scab, as some are saying they will, the escalation that will certainly follow will result in scenes in Notts far beyond those seen to date. The media this week have been unbelievable in their treatment of us: we have had more coverage in our favour this week than in practically the whole of the dispute. Hopefully this is the beginning of the final push. It may take a week or two yet; but what the hell, after all this time.

Thursday 18 October
We have the start of a move to change the Notts Area rule book. If successful, after deleting all reference to the National Union they hope to be a totally independent Area union. This way they have access to our Area fund and also our Area offices. Today is also the start of Maggie and Mac's media offensive to try to split NACODS; the Midland Area are now reconsidering taking action next Thursday. First plant the germ of an idea and then nurture it … they have a full week to do this. This tactic is so obvious and yet it seems to be ignored by all and sundry. This I do know: a lot of scabs and potential NACODS scabs are now shitting bricks at the prospect of this strike coming off. My feelings remain the same – the man who expects nowt is never disappointed.

Friday 19 October
Last night's flyer saw Ollerton as target; although the police outnumbered the lads, they were charged with truncheons because they wouldn't allow themselves to be encircled. A van was overturned, fights broke out and ten lads were arrested.

One of the arrested was Mick McGinty, our Area strike treasurer. Because of his sensitive position as a Notts Area leader, common sense should have kept him away – but I could understand his feelings and the need to be involved.

That weekend we received information that at first puzzled us: large amounts of coal were being moved through Clipstone at the weekends. Both the origin and destination were something of a mystery; we set up a surveillance of the Baulker Lane area of the village. What we found astounded us: coal was being unloaded on the railway sidings towards Old Clipstone during the week and then on to lorries at the weekend. Which pit it came from we never did find out, and the destinations could have been just about anywhere: the difficulty was knowing what to do about the situation.

It was becoming increasingly clear that Roy Lynk and his cronies were preparing the ground towards an eventual breakaway in the Notts coalfield. The proposed rule book changes were being put into practice on the advice of lawyers who were present at the Notts Area offices on an almost live-in basis. The crunch time, we were advised, would be the November branch meetings when the invited rule changes would be put forward to the Area Council meeting.

Sunday 21 October

Branch meeting at 10am – a pretty fair turnout from our lads but a very poor attendance from the scabs. We had anticipated being swamped, given M's efforts to whip up feeling against us; having said that, we were still easily outnumbered. Discomfort for him when we forced a vote he nearly lost asking for cash to help with the electricity bill at the centre. A reasonable discussion on the proposed change of rules: we managed to plant the idea, we think, in a lot of minds of the true implications of this action – we have to keep the lawyers out and the Notts Area within the National Union. Pleased today that the lads for tomorrow's collection in Nottingham have organised themselves today; I'm sending twelve of them and if I get wrong over it, then it was done with the best of intentions.

The Coal Board today are really running scared. They have now decided to take Mac out of the limelight and replace him with Michael Eaton, former Yorkshire Area director. He has started off well for us by calling for another ballot of NACODS. Who the bloody hell does he think he is conning with this sort of talk? They balloted only about three weeks ago and achieved an 82 per cent majority for strike. NACODS meeting tonight at Clipstone was reported to be unanimous for strike; same result reported from Rufford while Mansfield has decided to heed the call. While I'm not at all happy that it looks like being the deputies who can bring this dispute to a head, I'll be quietly excited if it comes off.

Monday 22 October

These Monday mornings soon come round. The usual ones turn up regularly; if only we could get a little more commitment on this shift. Police are from Essex; they've been here a few times before, not always with the same men – what is clear is that they don't relish it now the weather is turning, standing in any sheltered place they can find. No trouble this

116

morning – abuse to us by the scabs is ignored by them. 'Silver Birch' has surfaced again: he is supposedly taking out an injunction against the deputies alleging that their strike, if it happens, will be illegal. How much more shit will these bastards be allowed to stir up? Our tactics should be to try to discredit these traitors in the eyes of both the public and the Union membership.

B Herbert stopped a lorry this afternoon and attempted to talk with the driver. He was dragged away from the cab and threatened with arrest; we are used to this sort of thing, but that doesn't make it legal. A very disheartening and sickening event this afternoon when a bag containing cash and the ladies' section bank book was missed after dinner; a thorough search proved fruitless and we are left with the thought that we possibly have a thief amongst us. After all we've been through together, we don't want to believe this and I still hope the missing articles will turn up. The first casualty will be this week's food parcels – the ladies cannot withdraw cash without the book, while it seems about £60 is the amount lost in cash. Talks tomorrow at ACAS between NACODS and the Board: it looks as though a buy-off is on the way.

Tuesday 23 October
Just made it to the picket line this morning but had to be brought straight back to the centre; both back and neck causing problems so I look like being in collar and corset at least for today. News that is going to dismay the lads: the picket money looks like being cut next week from 75p to 50p. The problem is that cash from outside fundraising is drying up and, as we have no Area cash available to us, this is our sole means of financing a picket payment. If it dries up altogether, with what we get from National for petrol, WE ARE DEAD! Our collection yesterday realised £114. After deducting £24 expenses, I was hoping for a better result. I'm not taking anything away from the work put in as we realise a limited amount of cash is available anyhow; with collections taking place seven days a week, it probably counts as a really good score. Thanks, lads.

Wednesday 24 October
Made it to the centre and decided to stay there. No such luck: by 5.25am I was called down to the picket as B had been arrested again. At 5.15am only three of the lads had arrived and were in the process of sorting themselves out, stood together with two constables. The Little Hitler in charge came along and immediately ordered B away; jokingly he replied: 'I'm a working miner.' Hitler bristled, ordered him away again and before he could do anything about it had him grabbed and taken away. This inspector told me bluntly he had no intention of discussing the matter. Our response, having only twenty-three against three vanloads in reserve, was limited to keeping them out an extra thirty minutes until 6.40am; the lads also took to walking backwards and forwards along the front of the baths. They were really angry. Just after 9am I found out from the police station that he was only to be cautioned; a massive relief as he is already on bail on two charges. We had him home by 10am.

Later the result that we had all been expecting came through: NACODS had been bought off, like all the rest. On this occasion, however, their own vested interest should have been enough to bring them with us: redundancies will come to deputies just as they will to us. We are getting some support from within the power stations, but it is too little and the impact isn't dramatic enough; our thanks, though, to those inside and the railwaymen who are doing what they can in difficult circumstances. I feel a growing desperation, as if our efforts are not going to be enough. Perhaps it's the way that I'm feeling at present: my thoughts are becoming noticeably more morbid. It gets harder!

Thursday 25 October
Talks today between the NUM and the Board at the offices of ACAS went on all day but the result was almost inevitable. Now NACODS have sold out, the Board will be seeking to turn whatever screws they can. With the sequestration also working at National funds, Mac is probably feeling things are looking favourable for him. News for you, fella – your guns just ain't big enough. That said, if the weekly allowance for petrol and mileage dries up, it's difficult to see how we can finance it elsewhere. A complete rethink of the whole scheme of strike finance in Notts is now needed urgently.

Friday 26 October
Still hors-de-combat but frustrated rather than depressed: I've lost touch with what's going on at both the centre and the picket line. I also missed the picket managers' meeting yesterday; keeping in touch at that level is so important to me. Scargill meeting the TUC today, but nobody has stomach for the fight. If we were to lose this, then Maggie's victory would be complete. So far she's been able to bully and buy her way through – all except the NUM.

Sunday 28 October
We have to work doubly hard against the lads becoming demoralised; when they realise the picket money is cut and that nothing is coming from National level, it will be an extra test of their support and determination. If we do not suffer more losses on Monday morning, I'll be very surprised.

Latest media 'go' at us today is saying that Libya's Gaddafi has been approached for support. This is to help prove their charge of the political left-wing nature of the strike.

Monday 29 October
I expect the lads who have gone to Nottingham for the collection to have some shit thrown at them due to the 'disclosure of the Libyan connection' – how bloody skilful Maggie's puppets are at directing the shit to their best advantage. Ill-advised as it certainly was, we must keep things in perspective. Certainly we want nothing from Libya at any price, but when it is remembered that something like fifty countries have been visited by invitation, the hysteria caused by the media is unwarranted, to say the least. This sort of publicity can do harm in many ways: besides losing us financial support from the borderline cases, it also undermines the morale of the lads.

On ITV tonight *World in Action* showed what we have been saying all along: that the policy of this Government is to privatise the coalmining industry of these islands. Denials persistently made at the outset of the dispute are not even thinly disguised now. Just how much convincing does the working class of this country need? The danger for us now is that 'she' still has plenty of time before the next General Election to put through all the privatisation legislation that she cares to.

This was a period when all hell broke loose, with stories reported in the most lurid and emotive detail of these emissaries of the strikers paying court to Colonel Gaddafi in their efforts to raise cash for our National hardship fund. By becoming 'involved' with people of the reputations of the Libyans, we appeared to have given our opponents the biggest stick imaginable with which to beat us. The reality of the situation was that the visit was by Roger Windsor, NUM chief executive officer from 1983–89, and whose treachery to our Union was well-documented at a later date by Seumas Milne in his book *The Enemy Within*. It should be realised that those operating abroad were doing so at the invitation of trade unionists in the countries concerned; as for the Libyan connection, this, to my knowledge, was down to Windsor himself and was viewed by many, including myself, as a huge mistake.

The hypocrisy of the outbursts that were raised by right-wing politicians and journalists was nothing short of disgraceful. The fact that many senior Tory politicians had direct contact with British companies that were doing millions of pounds' worth of business with the Gaddafi regime was not even worthy of a mention. A trade union, on the other hand, that dared to make contact with an 'untouchable' risked being put to the literary sword.

Tuesday 30 October

Happily the picket money was not cut today as expected: a better week of fundraising has eased the situation – but only just. The team in Belgium, which includes one of our ladies, had a good response, although two of them were at one point arrested by the police there. They were not charged. It seems the Belgian miners are also contemplating strike action any time. Our Area legal advice centre is now firmly established despite the efforts of the scabs, Law Society and various others to sabotage it. Besides legal advice we also have access to benefit help and advice: for example, representing our interests at hearings, coordinating claims and appeals for family income supplement. More than usual amount of abuse experienced by the lads collecting today thanks to the 'Libyan connection'; plus it meant they only took £66 before deducting expenses – this from eleven men.

Wednesday 31 October

Police Watch arrived at 8am this morning to help us to establish a picket line at the Area stores. The police were on the scene within five minutes. With our lady friends present, one with a camera and another taking notes, the inspector conceded that an injunction was needed to remove us – the first time they have backed off.

In the meeting after dinner I suggested a strict rota to cover the picket; no one objected, although some did not look too keen. We finish this week on a voluntary basis and start next week with the rota. Problems of an individual nature can be sorted out when the sheet goes up; I hope that if we can turn lorries quickly, their appetite for action will return.

119

Thursday 1 November

Area stores rota well-established and working well: this morning lorries were being turned away that had previously gone in unchallenged. Production figures for one week in September: overall in Notts it is down by 30 per cent. For Clipstone the figures are down from 20,000 tonnes to just over 8,000. These are the Coal Board's own figures.

L of Sherwood is facing problems: when he suspended all Sherwood lads on strike without consulting his committee he little realised it would lead to him being isolated by his fellow scabs; on top of that he now has to extricate himself from a financial investigation by his branch. Our old friend Sid Richmond appeared before the welfare management committee to put his case against M for the abuse and threats he made against him the other week; it seems the meeting broke up in disorder when M refused to vacate the chair while the complaint was heard.

Friday 2 November

Day shift started – on my birthday – with the kitchen being unmanned yet again. Jim Dowen came up from the picket line and together we made a breakfast. The toothache I've had these last few days is now unbearable. Young C Hood was the first to the pit and was standing outside the car park entrance: two of the big brave Met bully boys came out and asked him if he was a picket; they stood one on each side of him and started to jostle him, then stood on his toes and told him to fuck off.

The appeal tribunal for our lad's special diet allowance has been upheld – another small victory for us. The situation overall seems to be that the Board are making a push against Derbyshire and pits on the Derby/Notts border. A lot of effort has gone into the scheme which has seen <u>all</u> levels of senior management visiting the lads <u>at their homes.</u> The determination by the Board, police and Government to break this strike is shown by the collusion that they now do not try to hide. This afternoon's announcement to strikers gives the impression that a £650 bonus payment will be made to anyone going back to work. This is a complete misrepresentation of the facts: the sum is made up of holiday money which is already due to the lads under statute plus the Christmas holiday period which is also theirs as of right. This is the lowest and meanest of tricks: it is nothing short of blackmail where the lads with kids are concerned.

Monday 5 November

Lads thin on the ground at the picket line – this I expected, with the new rota starting today. Last minute filling in and changing over kept me busy until afternoon shift. Area stores rota cocked up first day when the second pair didn't show up. One of them unfortunately started back; he was one of the single lads and I'm not feeling too confident about his mate, also single.

£8 million worth of National funds traced to Dublin and frozen until a hearing. Gut feeling is that this will be upheld. It seems our Area funds have also been frozen, with banks instructed not to accept cheques handed out to the ladies groups. More pressure today when the lads started to receive individual letters from the manager inviting them to an interview. He wants to discuss their position with them. Any of the lads who went to see him also found a handwritten note waiting for them with details of what they had to come if they started back; pressures we don't seem able to counter.

Policeman monitors Clipstone Colliery car park entrance *(News Line)*

Tuesday 6 November

We now know that we lost four back to work yesterday. One was getting near to retirement and two were single lads. I really do have sympathy for their position, but to go back now without any guarantee of an agreement is very silly, considering all they have suffered so far. Both gate rotas working smoother today with a load of electrical equipment and a BOC lorry turned away. Problems have taken up quite a bit of time today and one in particular was a threatened eviction. This case threw up a new aspect of housing benefit: if a single lad lives at home, even though he is on strike and over eighteen and not in receipt of any supplementary benefit, his parents' rent rebate is cut by £8.88.

A call tonight from IL, Burnley, asking me to go there to speak on November 22nd; he's trying to get Gerald Kaufman to speak and wants someone to help 'pad out'. His idea is for someone involved at first hand with the police activity, as the subject is to be the new police bill and how it affects the Labour movement. Bearing in mind all that IL has done for us, I could not refuse. Now I'm lumbered.

The absurdity of the 'wigs and masks' situation reached even greater proportions around this time. As well as rushing the heavily armoured Transit vans through the pit gates at speed with a police escort, cardboard cut-outs were at times sat in the seats to make it look as if more men were on board than was the case. The early morning runs were varied in terms of route and time to frustrate our response; the whole thing taking on a cloak-and-dagger appearance one would normally associate with a wartime situation.

And the mad scramble for coal went on unabated. We were particularly interested in the companies involved in the 'growth industry' of pulling coal through picket lines; as closely as we monitored this, however, our list was incomplete as many of the vehicles entering were unmarked; many of these must have been taken from the scrapheap as they were literally falling to bits. When the incomplete count reached fifty-four, we saw the size of the mountain facing us.

The greed of individuals at that time was exemplified by a chock fitter employed at Clipstone. At the end of his shift he was coming out of the pit and taking over the wheel of his father's lorry to pull coal through picket lines. To add insult to injury, he was crossing the picket at his own pit; our complaints to the branch officials and thereafter to the full branch meeting, and our demand for action to be taken against him, resulted in him almost receiving a medal from some of the 'working' branch members. With the total lack of will to uphold our complaint, we decided it was time we took action ourselves: we recorded, to the minute, the handover from his father and the routes and destinations of the loads he was carrying. I paid a visit to the local income tax office to acquaint them with his extra-curricular activity; nothing was done secretly and along with the information about the driver, I provided the office with my own identity and details, telling them we would be happy to cooperate if they needed witnesses. I am not, by nature, the kind of person who would involve himself in people's affairs, but in this case we had pulled the plug on an adversary who was without conscience – and I was very happy about it.

Wednesday 7 November

Fleet lorries we've not seen before were today coming through the picket continually; surprisingly there have been a number of fresh Yorkshire firms involved this week, particularly from the Barnsley and Rotherham area. One driver yesterday made the excuse that his firm would lose their contract with the Coal Board if he refused to cross our picket. Don't believe it.

After McGinty's complaints about the number of lads we've been sending, one car, three lads away to Nottingham for our collection. They returned later in the afternoon, having taken £24. Thick skins are needed there – it's no place for anyone of a sensitive nature.

Thursday 8 November

Tonight we watched a programme on BBC2 dealing with the activities of the police in the dispute. The film was made by Sheffield Police Watch; it showed film and interviews made mainly in Yorkshire of incidents of police violence on the picket line. Watching it, many incidents both seen and reported to me by the lads were brought back to my mind. The massive police presence, intensive patrolling both on foot and in transit, the abuse, threats and, in some cases, physical assault – these are memories that will live forever. One pleasing aspect in the film was the appearance of the probation officer at the Mansfield courthouse; I've had some contact with this gentleman and am impressed by his sincerity. The fact that he appeared tonight increased my respect for him. He has put his career on the line for our cause.

Friday 9 November

Two more active lads, and one who is not active, are talking of going back to work on Monday. They need working on this weekend but as the trend at present is the drift back, they'll need some convincing. Two scab joiners came out to fix a sign to a wall and I became involved in an argument with one of them; I was threatened with arrest 'because of my attitude'. I told the officer concerned that his ears were too sensitive.

Our friends at Cortonwood are having it rough at present: one scab went into work yesterday and today the pit was the target for the Yorkshire Area. The police were there in force; the lads were charged with horses and riot squads but held their own. The unfortunate thing is that the police and authorities now rely on the desperation and frustration of the lads as an excuse for mounting a campaign of 'retribution'; they are now realising that these measures are counter-productive, as they may get a few scabs into work, but long-term damage is being done to public confidence in policing methods.

Saturday 10 November

Picket managers' meeting called at Ollerton to tell us that National are ordering us back on the Trent Valley power stations. They are now to fund the operation as we cannot. Rotas were arranged for the three stations on a 24-hour basis; Clipstone was not included as I need to establish our gates and also an understanding with the lads. Our active picket is going down each week – we are now down to fifty-four.

Sunday 11 November

Bad news today when another lad phoned me to say that he was going back to work on Monday. That makes four that we know about. All of them have been talked with, but I fear that their minds are made up.

Monday 12 November

Black Monday, morale-wise: five lost to us. Most of these were the result of pressure from their wives; while the women have been the backbone so far, it is now they who are forcing the lads back. I cannot criticise some of them, knowing the domestic pressures, but I feel very sad nonetheless. Dentist today, so no dinner picket for me – the bloody thing is still giving me gyp.

Trouble right across Yorkshire, with the media having a field day. Mick Carter at Cortonwood told me tonight of the sort of misreporting we have been subjected to today: the shop reported as being broken into and looted has, in fact, been closed for seven months.

Tuesday 13 November

Day shift just covering the picket again; same old procedure that has demoralised the lads for so long. We might just as well not be there for all the effect we have on the scabs. Superscab M struts along the front of the baths just like the big-hitter he fondly imagines himself to be. The lads told him today he was full of nothing but shit; his response was to grin.

Cortonwood delegate Mick Carter at Clipstone strike centre *(John Lowe)*

Some figures of Board losses for South Notts so far show this must be the most expensive coal ever mined; the amount lost at five of the pits ranges from £6.5 million to £24.5m. How much money are they prepared to spend to try and crush us? The real crunch for us has been the weather: until it breaks, the position of the generating board will not become apparent. My fervent wish is for blizzards and a freeze-up; second best would be blanket fog. Anything to bring things to a head! A Notts County Council social worker came today to let us know that the under-five-year-olds now qualify for a clothing grant. Too little, too late! The school year started over two months ago. The sloths have finally woken up to the fact that there is a hell of a lot of hardship about.

Wednesday 14 November

The drift back continues, with two more giving in this morning. The situation at Clipstone is not good. On the one hand there are domestic pressures; on the other panic when the Board announce their Mickey Mouse figures. Later this morning, a rare treat for both myself and my dog: a walk in the woods. An oasis of peace in an otherwise mad existence packed with turmoil.

Thursday 15 November

Today the ladies took the initiative in trying to boost the lads. They have always taken the view, and rightly so in my opinion, that money sent to the kitchen is to be spent on food; this week however they decided that circumstances are exceptional and gave out £3 with every food parcel. I think they were spot on.

The National Executive Committee meeting today reaffirmed their commitment to the principles of the strike. What I want from them is a better thought-out strategy to overcome the bad press that we have come to expect. Right from the start too much emphasis has been placed on the big rally while the soft underbelly of Notts was virtually ignored; now we are paying the price.

Friday 16 November

Reports today of fighting at a neighbouring pit between those returning to work and those who have scabbed all the way through, with the result that several have been sacked and injured. North Derbyshire have heard of it, but have been unable to substantiate it so far. What is clear is that the numbers returning in Derbyshire are way below the figures given by the Board, e.g. at Markham 128 as opposed to the Board's 300–400 and Ireland Colliery twelve against twenty-eight. It really is heartbreaking to see lads who have taken everything so far walk in the back way rather than pass our lads on the picket lines.

Tommy Taylor, the ASLEF[11] branch secretary from Shirebrook, gave us a very comprehensive talk on the activities of his own branch depot and the one at Worksop. The signalmen, he said, were the key to any effective operation, and it seemed that at Shirebrook we did not have their support. The signalmen at Worksop, on the other hand, had been very supportive of our cause, despite being out on a limb. Their actions to date ensured the Trent Valley stations were starved of coal and were desperate for supplies to be brought in: Cottam and West Burton had virtually nothing coming in by rail and depended on convoys of lorries. The Clipstone Branch was invited to lobby a meeting of the Worksop Branch of the NUR[12] to try to bolster support; despite my exhortations, there was no inclination at Area level of the NUM to encourage these actions or even offer them as a subject for discussion. On reflection, we suffered from many blind spots.

Also that week, TUC boss Norman Willis had a rough time in Wales when he condemned violence in front of a miners' support rally. How he expected to get away with that I don't know. Neil Kinnock also came under fire at local level, with his own party demanding his resignation and expulsion from Labour. This was a bit drastic, but understandable given that he had consistently distanced himself from us over the months – I speculated at the time that he was out of the same mould as Concannon.

Monday 19 November
We had been told that more were going back this morning; in fact, we had four lads returning to work, none of whom had been picketing on a regular basis. This does not lessen the feeling of dejection when it finally happens. Life and the strike must go on.

Last night IL called from Burnley to say that everything was set up for Thursday. It seems that I am to be the only speaker there. The idea is to show videos of the police actions and for me to speak on the tactics employed by the police. This should be a piece of cake, but I still haven't prepared anything. I must get down to some work on it – there's not much time left. I'll be sleeping at PC's, I'm told, and this I'm looking forward to – if he has his homebrew ready, anything can happen.

Tuesday 20 November
Power station rota not being kept up by some pits – Rufford seems the main culprit and they have been taken off this week's rota. Clipstone will try to cover 10am–6pm Saturday and Sunday this coming weekend in Sherwood's place. This is the only cover we might manage at present; I wanted to be off the Area stores, but was told to stay with it. So be it.

Wednesday 21 November
Only seven at the pit gates this morning. That I wouldn't mind if we could rely on it. I'd be satisfied with a token picket if it was done in rotation; unfortunately it's the same men. Some of these H Division Met boys look hard buggers and ready for trouble – real hardened veterans. I'm still waiting to see their Y Division, and No. 42 in particular.

Strike meeting after dinner and something of a blood-letting – the noisiest yet. I'm afraid I didn't conduct it very well and lost my temper also. Main subject was the picketing and our need to make more commitment. Certain ones are not keeping with the rota, thus making it rough for those waiting to be taken off. The row centred on the Nottingham collections and our 'grounded crew', or certain ones objecting to having to bear the brunt of this job. My response was that our first priority is picketing and if this job means taking lads away from the picket, I was quite prepared to scrub the collection. This upset quite a few, who obviously had a vested interest. In the end everything was sorted amicably and hopefully some of them have something to think about.

Maggie has just topped all her previous efforts: she is raising the £15 supposed strike pay deduction from supplementary benefit. From a week next Monday £16 will be deducted to 'keep in line with inflation'. If this doesn't prove one of her most spectacular own-goals, the British working class will stand for anything.

Thursday 22 November

When a Euro MP from the Manchester area[13] visited us at lunchtime, she expressed surprise at the mood prevailing at the centre and was very impressed both by the efforts of the ladies and the attitude of the lads. They really have been great given the terrible start to the week. By 4pm we were on our way to Burnley for the public meeting tonight at 8pm.

It was well-attended and the crowd very receptive to my speech; I had hoped that more questions would be asked, but they seemed well-satisfied. If I do this sort of thing again, I need to get more punch into the message. In this meeting I had thought that the quiet, dispassionate approach would be the best, but now I'm not so sure: when preaching to the converted, the need is to make them angry. We saw a fair bit of the Burnley lads, visiting their strike centre later. As things stand they are 'quids in' compared to our lads;

Clipstone strikers in good spirits next to the 'green' *(John Lowe)*

if ours knew their full circumstances, I'm afraid that I'd have a mutiny on my hands. Financially, their situation seems such that they can get as much in one day as ours get in a whole week.

When the extra £1 deduction from supplementary benefits was announced, uproar followed in Westminster. Some of the Labour MPs blocked the aisles and wouldn't let the debate continue; they are seeking an emergency debate. Typical of Maggie's mob is that this was only announced in a written reply to a question on the subject. Stick in there, Skinner boy: we don't seem to have too many friends who are willing to stand up and be counted these days.

Friday 23 November

After a very late night plus PC's hospitality, D Huzij wasn't feeling good. He's now sworn off beer! Our friends loaded the car with second-hand toys for our kids – and a good selection they are. They have spread our list of kids amongst the wards of the constituency so it looks like they'll all be receiving a present, gift-wrapped with their names on. Good show!

The weekend saw the visit of our friend from the Manchester area who we knew as 'Chad'. Our only other knowledge of him at that time was that he was some sort of chef and that he seemed a very educated fellow. As we got to know him better we were to learn that he was in fact an hotelier on the outskirts of Manchester and that everything he brought us over in that period was a personal gift from himself and Flo, his wife. This was substantial and gratefully received; but almost as important was the fact that we came to regard them as personal friends. Chad had turned up at the kitchen one day with his car full of food and a cash donation – and thereafter cheques arrived periodically for the women's section. On this occasion he brought Christmas decorations for the strike centre, food to add to our Christmas stock and a bloody great tray of hotpot for the next day's dinner. Whenever he came he kept us enthralled with his knowledge of events past, his understanding of present-day happenings and his forecasting of what would happen on many other subjects – one hell of a character.

During December we had visits from Pendle and Whitby to bring donations of food and clothing. In the beginning, it was perhaps understandable that many showed a reluctance to take second-hand clothes; by the autumn, however, we were long past having such sensitive ideas. With the quality of that being donated, we were indeed very fortunate and made good use of what was on offer. The food coming through in increasing quantities was helping boost our stocks for Christmas while toys were also being brought: with almost a hundred kids to cater for, our supporters gave us hope that they would not go short come Christmas. One mother at our centre solved family worries that they could not provide for their daughters by promising them that they would have a special celebration later – Christmas celebrated at Easter. The kids were really thrilled at the thought.

Sunday 25 November

Branch meeting this morning – superscab M really had his legions out for this one. We are told he had put the word around that he was to try to lift the overtime ban. I think it's only a matter of time before this happens somewhere in the Area, but we have to resist while ever we can. Amendments to rule changes were supposed to be on the agenda but were not even mentioned in the delegate's report, so presumably none were submitted from branches. The Area Executive does not want its list of ten confused with others that might have been submitted: this seems to be an unconstitutional procedure, to say the least. In last month's branch minutes an extra rule was supported but never appeared in the delegate's report – another slip-up? Sooner or later they'll hang their bastard selves. We also have to decide how to deal with another blatant attack: among our lads are three pit inspectors and Sid Walker has taken it upon himself to sack them all and elect three others in their place. He didn't even have the decency to inform the lads in a proper manner. One he contacted by phone on Friday, one he approached direct and the third one was told this morning. Disgraceful – a breach of both rules and any decent way of conducting Union business. Walker has now shown his true feelings, thinking the die is cast for our defeat. Another – do they never cease? – incident, this time involving the double scab F. The meeting voted overwhelmingly for the branch to take no action despite this swine crossing picket lines and driving coal, we are told since before the overtime ban began. Again a decision that at some future date will, we hope, rebound on them. This is still not finished with! M again coming out with the shit – I'm amazed he is able to muster support. He is barred from the club for three months but can enter to conduct his duties as a trustee; he also has to appear before the welfare committee again because of his arrogant disregard for the ban imposed by them. He was drinking and boasting he couldn't be stopped because of who he is – this on the very night following the ban. There's no end to what he thinks he can get away with.

Monday 26 November

Day shift with a difference: the only copper in sight was the one in the control car. We quickly realised that the difficulties that they face elsewhere have meant the withdrawal of forces from Notts. We now have to devise ways of getting them back again. Just after 11am the local fuzz came out and announced that no police would be coming to Clipstone this week; the lads then occupied the small green and doubled up along the front of the baths. The local copper sent for reinforcements; unfortunately for him, they didn't arrive until too late. Minutes after the lads left, a motorcycle rider led in a bus-full followed by a car full of 'brass'. This made my day as they know what will happen if they leave us unattended: when the cat's away, the mice will play.

Nationally the shit continues to fly. Maggie says she'll never negotiate with 'men of violence'. The truth is we're not supposed to be negotiating with her, but with the Board. It's no wonder the lads get angry and frustrated. If some of them did not hit back now and then, that would be the surprise.

Tuesday 27 November

Surprise: numbers up to fourteen this morning and still only the control car in attendance. He tried a little run at the lads for standing more than two to a gate but then retired to his own little spot. He's like a rat peeping out. Best description I've heard of the police yet: 'They're like wolves. When there's one he stands off and watches. When there's two they close in a little and still watch. When there's three they attack.'

Picket managers meeting at Ollerton: rota decided with Clipstone to maintain cover for Sherwood on Saturday and Sunday at West Burton. Notts's commitment to 24-hour cover at the Trent Valley power stations is proving expensive, both in cost and in men: total active pickets in the Area now down to around 1,000.

Wednesday 28 November

This morning we have been successful in pulling back the police: we had one Transit van full of Notts men and a busload, we think, of the Met. For six men on the picket line, this is the level of protection we need; if this were repeated throughout Notts, it would certainly ease things for our brothers elsewhere. Ray Chadburn, who I've been trying to get hold of for days now, finally called me yesterday afternoon and it seems he did tell Walker to discuss our scab driver at the Branch meeting. He claims there are no sanctions he can take. He also said he had ordered Walker to investigate breaches of the overtime ban and stop them. I'm afraid that Walker, cohorting with Lynk as he does, will not do much about it.

A crisis tonight when the ladies' section chairwoman and secretary came round with all their books and announced they had resigned. After a lot of talking I hope they will let things lie for a couple of days before making a final decision. This should not be my headache, but the ladies of late have not been as tightly organised as they ought to be: petty squabbles have been allowed to build up without a meeting to clear the air.

Thursday 29 November

Low turnout again for the day shift, but at least the kitchen staff turned up. Police presence was almost nil. Two Met boys joined us later after we sent the local off quick style for lecturing us on what we could and could not do outside the Area stores. Our attempts to speak to drivers are not unreasonable – and they gain nothing through denying us that with threats and intimidation. Food parcel today: I would like to see a little fresh meat now and again, but sausage is better than nothing.

Word this afternoon that 'working miners' should be sought who will be willing to sign to say they wish to remain within the NUM. Talk is of a writ to be prepared and served, I understand, on our scabby Area leaders and their like. I don't know if anything will come of this, but it didn't take me long to get four.

Friday 30 November

Afternoon shift reasonably well-attended but Friday is always a demoralising day when the scabs are drawing their thirty pieces of silver. And the story persists about Mansfield scabs going into Yorkshire, which has set me thinking of our own pit: certain notable scabs have not been showing up lately. There's a rumour – only a rumour, mind, and too much of this has already been put about – that a COSA[14] member checking wage packets noticed some were specially marked and found that they were payments for certain Mansfield Colliery lads who had been working in Yorkshire. More of the ones who have gone back have been asked if they would be prepared to sign their name to stay in the NUM; so far no one has refused. If things go against us with the vote on rules, we have to start recruiting back right away. The High Court today put the receiver in charge of our National funds; the situation becomes more farcical by the day. The funds we have in Luxembourg that the court there has released could now be at risk; with other Area funds also under threat I even fear for the cash donated outside the Union – I wouldn't put it past the courts to try to seize that.

Tragedy today when a taxi driver was killed in South Wales. A concrete post was thrown on his cab as he was taking a scab to work. The Clipstone strike committee disassociate themselves from this sort of thing and I was pleased when Scargill did likewise. Nothing can ever justify acts like this and the sooner those responsible are caught, the better.

Notes

1. Home Secretary
2. Energy Secretary
3. Yorkshire NUM president
4. Members of the National Association of Colliery Overmen, Deputies and Shotfirers
5. Elected a Labour councillor following the strike once M had been deselected
6. British Association of Colliery Management
7. Sid and Norman Richmond won their case for wrongful arrest against Nottinghamshire police in 1988, settling out of court for £4,000
8. Conservative Party Think Tank
9. Don Concannon, 1930–2003, Labour MP for Mansfield
10. The family later pleaded guilty to being drunk and disorderly
11. Associated Society of Locomotive Steam Enginemen and Firemen
12. National Union of Railwaymen
13. Different to the one mentioned previously
14. Colliery Officials and Staff Association

PART FOUR

DECEMBER 1984–FEBRUARY 1985

Remarkably, considering the tactics of the Coal Board, the disgraceful attitude of the media, the drift back and that Christmas was looming, morale was very high both at Clipstone and reportedly throughout the Notts coalfield. The lads and their families could still raise a laugh and crack a joke.

Our logging team was working flat-out: Jim had negotiated with the manager of the Forestry Commission at Old Clipstone and had secured an area from which we could take away the dead wood. A charge of £10 had been made for this right and excellent value it proved to be, easing our fuel situation as it did. Our old friend Sid – 'the one they couldn't buy' – had initially set us up when he provided four bow saws; we had then acquired a petrol-driven saw supplied by the Notts women support group. In addition our own women had paid for a Land Rover to be put back on the road, the ideal vehicle for the rough work of bringing the fuel out of the forest.

The calls upon our manpower from the various commitments were by now well-nigh intolerable. We were committed to three change-of-shift pickets daily, had to provide lads for fundraising away from home whenever the call came from the Area strike committee while our own weekly collection in Nottingham also had to be considered a priority. The women's section required drivers several times a week for food pick-ups and the logging teams were in the forest every single day. In preparation for the trials of those arrested, witnesses needed transporting to our legal centre at short notice to make statements, and on trial days the accused and their witnesses had to be taken to wherever their charade was taking place. Flying pickets played a big part in the strategy of the Notts strikers and there were many other one-off commitments too numerous to list: it could be said that we were too busy to realise how desperate our situation was becoming.

Sunday 2 December

Young J, our friend from Pendle doing the sponsored bike ride for us, arrived earlier than expected yesterday and was remarkably fresh. He stayed with J Taylor and saw a few of the lads in the evening. He then left this morning just after 9am: I don't envy him his task, cycling upwards of 100 miles twice in two days – not my idea of fun. The possibility of an injunction against Notts Area on the rule changes continues to dominate my thoughts today. List prepared of names who have said, or who we think would be prepared to, sign to this effect. Later in the evening the text of the form was given me – we will have to pull out all the stops tomorrow. Jim Hood, who could have helped us, is going to Scotland; the wisdom of this move I seriously question. With the special delegate meeting tomorrow and given our legal position and lack of direction at this time, all of our own leadership should be here helping to maintain what we have.

Monday 3 December
The 7–9am shift at the pit gate and a bloody cold wind we had; it also pissed down – a hard exercise with no shelter or fire to keep us warm. Still the lorries keep coming and the stock seems to be higher than normal. I suspect the bunkers have been emptied this weekend, but we cannot prove this. After the gate, had to dash off to Berry Hill to get a draft of the form typed up and copied; just made it back for the afternoon shift. The response was better than I expected with more signing our paper than refusing. More would have signed if we had had time to talk to them all. As I'd hoped, a large body of opinion 'inside' does not want a Spencer union. Unfortunately a hell of a lot still do not realise the full implications of a vote in favour of change. We managed twenty-two 'working' and, along with our own signatures, upwards of fifty were taken through to Ollerton immediately after dinner to be sent to London tonight: the solicitors need them for tomorrow morning. We still cannot identify the house on Mansfield Road that was supposed to have been fired last week, another of the stories put out purely to cause us problems.

Late tonight the outcome of the special delegate conference in London: their decision is to carry on with the strike in its present form and to have nothing to do with the courtroom decisions. Their decision is strictly in line with the feelings of the rank-and-file on the picket line.

Tuesday 4 December
The Hampshire lot seem quick to move if they think we are not keeping to the guidelines. Good atmosphere in the centre for breakfast: when the lads from Thoresby and the logging team got back, it was like a bloody tap room.

The injunction has now been delayed by one week due to a cock-up. It might prove to be a blessing in disguise, giving us a chance to think it out better. The advice now is for legal aid applications to be filled in. We have something in excess of fifty complaints so this will be a problem.

One long night of phone calls and writing up till my bloody head was spinning. The injunction has put extra work on us that I hope will be justified.

Wednesday 5 December
Flyers were away to Shireoaks by 10am and it wasn't until 2.30pm that I learned they had been arrested in the village by the pit the moment they arrived – no chance to join the picket, therefore no chance to do anything wrong. On the face of it, they have grounds for wrongful arrest. These tactics are clearly designed to intimidate: if they are to be nullified then the lads have got to ignore and carry on. Problem is, after all this time we don't have so many lads available – or who haven't already been arrested. After the frantic phone calls

and dashing about of the last two days, we finally learned that the legal aid forms are now not needed. The solicitor is coming Friday to handle the situation herself. I'm relieved that we aren't rushing into it, but I consider it a liberty to have us chasing our arses for nothing. Finally got around to checking on the lads in court next week – and a good job I did. The records at Ollerton had not been altered from the original January date to 11th and 12th December. The solicitor will now contact them direct. The two in court on the 14th and 15th they seem to have in hand.

Thursday 6 December

My back has let me down completely and at present I'm more like a bloody cripple. I did manage to get to the centre this morning; shocked and disappointed when only three turned up for the picket. Commitment from most is pretty high but one or two ought to be doing a bit more.

Leaflets turned up just in time for the afternoon picket: we have to hope they read them thoroughly and act accordingly. Latest on the injunction: a call from London saying they now want only one signature for the writ. This they prefer to be from someone who has been working for some time. Again, I wish they'd decide what they want; having said that, I will go along with whatever is asked as far as is humanly possible. The writ must be served. Jim Dowen and myself visited an individual who is quite willing to do as we ask.

Friday 7 December

Solicitors now want me to get our subject down to London to talk with them. This is because of the pressures on them: they have a deadline next Wednesday on the writ served on our National leaders and this is taking almost all their time. Called subject and he readily agreed. Jim Dowen will probably drive him down, claiming expenses from the Forum. A call to Jim from Hull's King George Dock to say another £300 worth of food available to be picked up next week.

We picked up a Canadian from Mansfield who NUPE asked us to accommodate this afternoon. He is with a theatre workshop in British Colombia and is over here researching the dispute. He seems pretty clued up about world affairs and we both benefited from our long discussion. There are still lists to make up for NUPE: the single lads are to get something from them. A holiday in Belgium for the six-to-eleven-year-olds is also on offer. Names will go into a draw.

During the course of the dispute, we received many visitors at the Clipstone soup kitchen. We had people who had travelled from Canada, Australia, Italy, Germany and Poland. We welcomed young unemployed from London and a Euro MP from Manchester. Trade union officials came from London, Sheffield, Brighton, Manchester and many other places. There were those who travelled to Clipstone many times throughout the long months and all our support groups, in Whitby, Manchester, London, Burnley, Wellingborough and especially the Pendle constituency members, our greatest asset, deserve special mention. We were to receive many toys, as well as food, from all these groups, as well as a load from Watford, in the lead-up to Christmas.

Throughout the festive period, our position seemed at best just about financially viable. The post-Christmas period in prospect was however far bleaker: the reason was that so much of the support on the streets that we had been receiving was now being turned towards the many Christmas appeals being organised throughout the country. If we were to give our kids a decent Christmas, it had to be at the expense of what was to come later, despite the many donations to us. Although we never operated in any secretive way, it was decided to keep this news on ice for a while.

There were also those who visited us that were most definitely not welcome. These included almost all newspaper reporters and TV camera crews: interviews given in good faith to both TV and press were invariably distorted or plain ignored. On the day of my arrest, a 'Scandinavian cameraman' was giving close attention to all that took place and was very prominent on the photographs taken by our lads. Here, one might think, was the ideal witness for my defence; but when we needed to talk with him, he disappeared. They were not there to assist the cause of justice in any way.

Saturday 8 December

Preparations for social tonight going ahead at a rare pace. The arrangements are for a disco and bar, 50p admission charge with every lad on strike having his first drink free. A buffet is also being put on and a raffle will be held with some really good prizes.

The social went off fantastically. Snags when the bitter ran out – twice – because the room was full to bursting point, with a few friends from other groups. By the end of the night they were stood on tables and chairs singing; the lads just didn't want to go home. There was no trouble and everyone enjoyed themselves immensely.

Monday 10 December

An extended session this afternoon on the phone arranging for the five lads in court tomorrow at Renishaw: with two days set for the trial and the problem with witnesses who have returned to work, it wasn't as straightforward as it might have been. Luckily they still have some conscience: we finally got word that the three Clipstone witnesses were willing to go to court. Nothing we could do about the other two. In addition, the solicitor needs picking up at Chesterfield 8.30am. Two are also due in court Friday, and I'm now told that two of the witnesses need to make fresh statements as soon as possible; also that photographs taken at the scene are needed. I'm finding it difficult to keep up with happenings at National level: there are also so many writs flying about that keeping track of them is almost impossible. I'll really have to sort out my priorities – the problem lies in delegating any responsibility. I'm getting very tired and feeling shot at.

Tuesday 11 December

Picket managers meeting at 10am saw a lot of anger against the scabs expressed. The treachery against the National Union has caused bad feeling that, if we are not careful, could result in hasty decisions which could set us back further as an Area. Collections in

Nottingham continue to be abused by some pits: our lads yesterday were told by some there, who said they were from Creswell, that they would not cooperate and would go daily. This was denied by the Creswell picket manager. The question – or row – will be taken up by the Area strike officials once again tomorrow.

Wednesday 12 December
The five in court yesterday were bound over for six months in the sum of £50.

Thursday 13 December
On asking Ollerton for the court time tomorrow they had 2.30pm; a call to the magistrates' court put it at 10am. Good job I checked again – the lads would otherwise have been there without a solicitor. We need another court victory as a morale booster but somehow I'm very uncomfortable. Why would the magistrates choose to send our two to Mansfield and the third lad from Silverhill elsewhere? I would have thought it easier to try all three together, as they were arrested within minutes of each other. Some remarkable stories are unfolding of the efforts being made by people all over the country. The rank-and-file of the Labour and trade union movements have responded very generously as indeed have the general public. Much more sympathy is being shown than the media will tell. The harassment many of these groups face from the authorities when working on our behalf is disgraceful. People have been arrested and food and money confiscated. By what legal right? The writ! Statements have been prepared and affidavits sworn and tonight are on their way back to London. How soon it is issued now depends on our legal people.

Tonight on BBC2 our 'champion of the right to work', Chief Constable McLachlan, finally had to face people in the studio who were not prepared to be talked down to or browbeaten by his loutish attitude. He was savaged by Labour, SDP lawyers and others and he was so angry he lost his temper frequently. His true feelings towards us were made quite plain: I confidently predict that as a police spokesman he will now sink into obscurity as has his running mate MacGregor. He is becoming as big an embarrassment to the police as MacGregor is to the Board. Hasten the day when they both get their reward – the sack will suit them both!

Friday 14 December
The trip to Cortonwood tonight was called off at 2.30pm when Jim Dowen called to say that H was ill. My son-in-law in Rotherham came over and took me there. As the 'lone ranger' I could have had a very uncomfortable time, but not a bit of it: everyone there made me feel ten feet tall. The lads there from Leicester – the 'Dirty Thirty' – I now have a tremendous respect for. With just thirty from four pits on strike, they are doing a hell of a job. The River Don steelworkers who support the Cortonwood lads have also made donations to our centre; tonight they gave me a cheque for £160. They've also told me our ladies have to write in immediately and more cash could be available. Truly tremendous people. So many familiar faces, so many good wishes to bring back made a memorable evening.

The difference in police attitudes between 1972 and 1984 can be shown by the way strikers were treated then and now. In 1972 we were allowed to build a roadside shelter and to man the picket for twenty-four hours a day; we were also able to use a brazier both for cooking and warmth. Our right to picket and to speak to the drivers going in was recognised by all, including the police. Our numbers present at any picket could be anywhere between twenty and fifty and at Cottam power station – in 1972 a responsibility shared by Clipstone – the police even stopped the lorries going in to enable us to talk with the drivers.

In 1984, when we were able to get near the entrance to these places, our numbers were always restricted and we were called 'demonstrators' by the police; as such, we had no right to speak with any driver. If contact was, by some means, made with a driver, the kind of response from the police would be to invite the driver to 'piss off in' and the lads threatened with arrest. There were those who saw the threats of violence come to fruition: the lads often came back with stories of the police facing them with truncheons swinging, grinning aggressively – especially when the Nottinghamshire Constabulary was present.

Monday 17 December

Day shift picket reasonably well-attended: thirteen plus the two in the centre preparing breakfast. City of London police in attendance this morning and not bothering us; the only problem again was the bearded monster in the control car.

Tuesday 18 December

Good start to the day when I overslept and was nearly late for the flyers. Didn't make the pit but they were away by 6am. They were originally going to Shireoaks but a call last night changed that to Coalville in Leicestershire. This was in response to British Rail's decision to send two scab signalmen to start moving coal from there. Cock-up! The call, to be there by 7am, was well-supported by Notts – only to find it was, or should have been, 1.30pm. On the positive side, I think it has focused attention on our need to think about the movement of stocks more clearly.

Wednesday 19 December

Superscab M today walked into the centre and removed the cutlery, claiming that Jim Dowen and myself had agreed. The bastard has more face than is good for him: he lies and feels no shame that people know him for a liar. The old folks are having a Christmas party and need some of the equipment that belongs to the welfare; if asked, we would have handed it over readily.

Christmas presents for the kids distributed today and a very emotional time it was. Quite a few tears were shed, and not all of them by the mothers. Overwhelming!

Thursday 20 December

Bad morning: the power station flyers went late and with only two lads; along with the let-down in the pit gate rotas, I was just about ready to pack the job in on the spot. Later

I went to Ollerton to meet with a lecturer in law from Bristol University: he shared data showing police activity, arrest figures, court results. Although I was impressed, huge gaps were apparent and some of the figures used did not give an accurate account. So much of it depended on the solicitors acting for us returning details: in many cases they obviously had not. I was dismayed to find that our National leadership had not seen the need to institute such a survey from the outset and that it was not until around August/September that the present project was started. Its importance is in no doubt: only in this way can the media and Government collusion and distortion be proved.

Christmas food parcels were distributed today and really good ones they turned out to be: every family had a turkey plus a whole range of foods – traditional festive fare. The lads are overwhelmed by all this. On top of that the ladies gave every lad £5 plus £7 worth of vouchers. Jim Dowen went to Wakefield this afternoon for a debate on the dispute that was shown tonight. The studio audience was supposed to be made up of strikers and scabs, but many of the scabs didn't turn up; Jim spoke a few times and really made his mark. Unfortunately the people who should be watching programmes like this deliberately avoid having their consciences pricked.

Friday 21 December

Day shift well-supported: I'm told everyone was in good spirits. They are a great bunch of lads, despite my moans. Preparations were under way early for the kids' party this afternoon; with the ladies having such a busy day ahead, the lads decided to prepare the dinner – soup and bread. They were like big kids and seem to have the Xmas spirit. Time for the party finally came round and right from the start the place was bursting at the seams: not only the kids – around ninety – but mums, dads, grandparents and even the ones with no kids. It was so much more than a kids' party: a huge social evening enjoyed by everyone from the youngest to the oldest. There was a Santa, a snowman, a clown and something else impossible to describe; more gifts and chocolates were distributed, balloons by the hundred were burst and games were played – just! A disco then took over and everyone sang and danced to the finish. Not for one moment did the tempo and enthusiasm slacken and I, for one, was completely knackered by the end. What a great night; we now have a job of contacting and thanking everyone who has given us the opportunity to celebrate this festive season. Maggie, you should have been there to see just how beaten we are!

Christmas and New Year period

Flyers for the weekend power station picket, who had been paid for the job – 6am–2pm – on Friday, did not let me down. Saturday report that the fleet tankers are now openly crossing the picket and totally ignoring the lads; drivers have also been saying that our weekend cover was not maintained throughout the Trent Valley. Once again we are letting ourselves and everyone else down, considering the drivers' union told us that if we maintained a continuous 24-hour picket it would be respected. So often there are gaps in cover that we are unable to plug: the drivers naturally think that if we cannot fulfil our side of the bargain, then they feel no obligation to honour their promise.

Eight-man Clipstone picket at Bilsthorpe on Christmas Eve. We expected a good turnout but we were the only ones there. Where were the Bilsthorpe lads? Considering their pit was working, I consider this a disgrace.

Christmas card sent out by pickets *(John Lowe)*

Christmas Day and Boxing Day were days off for everyone, even the power stations.

Thursday, and a big day: our Christmas dinner at the Newlands community centre. Fifteen friends from Wellingborough and a family from Brighton were there to celebrate with us, including friends locally who have supported us throughout. A great time was had by all.

Friday and picket payout plus food parcels. Power station cover arranged for weekend plus gate rotas at the pit – a very satisfactory end to the week. After N Richmond appeared in court to answer a summons for 'traffic offences', his barrister then visited me at home; I was pleased for this chance to put the point across about legal people not returning the details of court cases often or quickly enough. He seemed genuinely surprised at the importance they should be placing on these records.

Power station Saturday – three fleet tankers plus scab brown ones went through: as some are coming more than once, they are obviously not travelling very far. The lads had a good look around: one side of the West Burton stocking ground has virtually no stocks: the existing heap had virtually no movement until around 5pm when three diggers came out and started moving coal. This seems to show total oil burn for the early part of the day, while no peak period is imminent. That being the case I suspect more oil than the tanker run is getting in.

On Sunday morning six Italians visited on a fact-finding tour of the British coalfields: they had been to Sheffield and Barnsley to make contact with the leadership and membership of

Lorry crosses picket line at West Burton power station *(News Line)*

our Union but, due to the holiday period, they had not met many of our people. On reaching Cortonwood, Mick Carter had a brainwave and put them in contact with our strikers: the lads gave them a great night and I think they were a little bewildered by the hospitality. I met them briefly on Monday morning before they left for London; apparently they had handed over £1,200 to the Yorkshire Area.

Wednesday 2 January 1985
Back to the grind with the alarm set for 4.15am. We must be bloody crackers. Seven of us turned up for the first picket and we were disappointed to find only one policeman on duty, the idle swines.

Thursday 3 January
Afternoon picket started off with a bang: by the time we arrived at the pit, the police were out in force. We took up our positions and nothing unusual happened until I walked across the road to jot down the tonnage figures. At this a cocky young bastard followed me and spoke as if to a dog. Because I showed resentment both he and his inspector threatened arrest; they are from Merseyside, arrogant and aggressive. At one point they were flashing £10 notes at us: if that isn't inciting trouble, I don't know what is.

Tried this afternoon to talk to some of the afternoon shift – as distasteful as it feels, it's the only fresh tack left open to us. One of the lads talked for fifteen minutes and was really sick of it – he would only promise to think about rejoining us and to talk to his wife. If we could get two or three out again, it would really boost the lads; unfortunately it would take a bloody miracle. Board and media campaign getting into gear now, with figures of 600 returns given for the last two days. Fucking liars!

Friday 4 January
The Merseysider and his mates were again eager for an excuse to dash in this morning: I was called 'shit-head' and 'fucking dick-head' almost simultaneously by two of them while a third almost had his finger up my nose, threatening arrest. This because I said to a scab: 'Good morning, snake.'

Picket managers' meeting at noon was long overdue. The importance of the power station picket being maintained and tightened up was highlighted: some picket managers are not playing fair or have lost a substantial amount of control over this issue. Also discussed was our present position relative to the strike: although we didn't get the injunction in the end, we still go back to court in three-to-four weeks' time. We were told that although it went against us first time, our case is still very strong. Regarding the scabs, we were assured that moves were being made to expel Notts from the National Union. It was pointed out that a special delegate conference would need to be called to achieve this. We were also told that the total assets of the Notts Area stood at £1.25 million. This figure seems hard to believe, but if true makes it no great deal to fight over. Our main task at that point will be to recruit back into a newly constitutionalised Notts Area union, within the National Union. We were told subs would be £1 a week. If our recruit back could achieve 5,000 membership then the scab union would need to charge £3 per week to stay solvent.

The lads told me later that while I was away they were subjected to physical threats and abuse: to 'smash your fucking face in' along with names such as 'shit-head' and 'wanker'; threats to arrest for shouting, no matter what the message; deliberately standing in front of the picket sign every time it was moved; and when asked if we had to stop breathing, the reply of: 'That can be arranged.'

Saturday 5 January

Meeting at Worksop, with Scargill speaking – packed hall as we expected. We were told later that a number of scabs were present. I hope that was true and that Arthur's speech had some effect on them: it was indeed powerful and he pulled no punches. It was aimed at the trade union movement generally and at the scabs in particular: he gave us a very comprehensive account of the situation, the failed ACAS talks and the future if we failed; his message to the scabs was made in a very quiet and emotional manner, urging them to avoid carrying 'the mark of Cain'. Surprisingly, though only briefly, the BBC showed Arthur delivering this message in part. ITV, on the other hand, chose to show him as he built up to make a point.

The snow we had prayed for finally came on the Monday. Until that time there had been hard rain and frost, but temperatures had not fallen for long-enough periods to cause problems at the power stations – which at that time of year one would expect. The gods were not with us! My prayers were for snow, ice, freezing fog – in fact anything that would cause increased oil-burn in the Trent Valley. We knew how pressured they were, but only adverse weather conditions would show the extent of this.

The second week in January proved to be another bad time for me in the physical sense. I was finding it increasingly difficult to keep pace with events and the needs of the day. We were on the threshold of matters that would decide the future of our organisation and we had to withstand what was thrown at us with all the strength we could muster. Had the strike been just the few weeks' sprint it was in the 1970s, I would not have been troubled unduly, but I was in no condition to weather the demands of a marathon.

Monday 7 January

A picket of twelve lads braved the snow that has finally come. It was bloody cold despite the extra layers I was wearing. The police, apart from having a look, left us alone. We have a problem at present, with two witnesses due to give evidence in two different cases on the same day. We have already been through this once, with a witness having to ask for a different date for his own case.

Night shift picket not very effective. Nine lads on the picket line and only one policeman in the control car with no reinforcements sent. Events now crying out for some night shift targets; if we don't get out in numbers, they won't even know we are there.

Tuesday 8 January

The question of the Notts Area's position within the National Union was discussed further at the picket managers' meeting at Ollerton. This time we were told our assets stand at £1.8m. The subject is to be on the agenda at the Executive meeting on Thursday in Sheffield – we are being asked to lobby the meeting to urge them to expel Notts. If they decide so, they will then call that special delegate conference to decide. We were told that 1st February would be the likely date such expulsion would begin. Back at Clipstone a meeting was held to put the lads in the picture; with the Area strike committee meeting Scargill at noon, Jim Dowen was not available. There was a vigorous debate and F Childs seemed upset at the prospect of Notts being expelled. His fears were shared by a handful of lads. They were told that it wasn't a matter where the rank-and-file in Notts now had a say, and the majority seemed to understand and go along with what was being suggested. I hope the doubts raised by this move, however inevitable, don't result in some of them going back. Arrangements were made for some of them to be at the lobby on Thursday.

Wednesday 9 January

Four cars and fifteen lads will attend the lobby at Sheffield tomorrow morning to demand their own expulsion from the NUM: it's a sobering thought. When this finally happens, we have to be in a position to defend the rights of our lads with the help of other Areas – that means the immediate formation of a new Notts Area of the NUM. May God go with us – we'll certainly be needing Him. Superscab F in court today on charges of burglary.[1] What a bloody turn-up: wonder if the media will give him as much prominence now as when he was 'championing the right to work' and starting legal action against his union.

Thursday 10 January

This week's rent-a-mob from Essex look a bloody big sample; they have been very quiet but take no chances and are out in force early. At breakfast we had twelve Kent lads to feed who are up for the lobby: they arrived last night and were housed in the village. Good set of lads, but to hear them talk, I'm afraid our exploits sound tame; I suspect though that away from home our lads would talk something similar.

At the meeting the scab Notts Area was warned that expulsion is being recommended, with a delegate conference called to make a decision; meanwhile talks of a kind will be held between scabland and the National Executive. Also decided was that any future negotiations with the Board would include the full Executive: this is a change of tactics by the leadership and must be because of pressure within the Executive. I am not dismayed by this at present, but I have a nagging fear that the moderates on the Executive will not be as insistent on our full demands as would the leadership.

Friday 11 January

The two supposed to be collecting never made it, a loss that we can ill afford: I sometimes think, perhaps unfairly, that no one's bothered until his own car needs money spending on it. In the last three weeks we've paid two full taxes and £40 on another four; cash is really tight. Another hardship case today, a mortgage problem: we've managed to give him some breathing space. We have, to my knowledge, four lads at risk: two are considering going back Monday and I feel the other two could follow.

Saturday 12 January

Power stations again the main discussion topic at the picket managers' meeting: with the Esso depot shop steward supporting us at present, we are not showing enough commitment. This week Rufford has let the rota at Cottam down and they were not present to explain why. We now have one week to tighten up.

Lads on the power station called to say the police had chased them off. At 7.10am, two tankers went through followed by a PSU,[2] which stopped; immediately the helmeted bully boys surrounded the car, searched it, kicked out the fire, questioned the lads and threatened to arrest them unless they went right away. The lads argued, but eventually left; from there they went to Cottam and found no one on picket at all. Instead of then staying at Cottam, they left and called at High Markham where they found the Mansfield Colliery lads in position. After all the talk this morning, it seems that Cottam and West Burton have been left totally without cover for almost the whole morning. All I could do was report in and alert the lads down to go tomorrow of what to expect.

Sunday 13 January

The same again: when the lads rang in at 7.10am, I asked them to return, but they were reluctant to without an observer. As one of them put it: 'It's not a very good feeling being surrounded by a bunch that size.' I asked two to stay by the phone while the other two drove back and observed whether tankers were going in. In the meantime, after some phoning around, I eventually spoke to an inspector at Epperstone police HQ: he agreed we had a right to be there and said he would send someone out to see the lads. He also asked if we wished to make a complaint: I told him not immediately, but when I had all the facts then we would possibly do so.

Yesterday's delegate conference at Berry Hill decided to suspend Henry Richardson, Area general secretary. They do not want him involved in meetings between now and a possible expulsion. What I don't understand is why Ray Chadburn, the Area president, chose to vacate the chair instead of committing himself: he has been under a lot of pressure, but he knows they don't want him and he's supposed to have been on our side throughout. His best interest would have been served by openly joining us. The *Notts Evening Post* already had the story printed yesterday morning, before the meeting actually took place; somehow Jim Hood got hold of a copy noon yesterday of last night's edition, printed and ready for distribution. The whole stinking rotten process sickens me.

Monday 14 January

Morning and afternoon pickets passed quietly. Although we are putting more lads across the front of the baths, these Essex lot are still not bothering us. Their boss has shown more common sense last week and today than we've seen for a long time. Two went back to work today; I could understand if they were the people under the most financial pressure, but unfortunately for us, we are now seeing ones whose wives are working giving up.

Meeting held to select three to start compiling a register for when we start recruiting back. The same fears were expressed: the contract of employment, the possibility of our being isolated and eventually sacked and the uncertainty because we are now coming on to new ground. I share these fears, but do not feel pessimistic in the least. According to Sherwood delegate Barry Smith, Richardson had a rough ride at yesterday's Area Council meeting with Chadburn resisting attempts to suspend him from the chair; the chair was then challenged, and after the vote Chadburn left the meeting. After legal advice, Henry maintained his right to the Area secretary position at today's Executive meeting; the differences were still being argued over at dinnertime.

This evening Lynk has plumbed new depths: he finally managed to get rid of Henry Richardson, Area general secretary. The fact that solicitors now sit in on every meeting at Berry Hill, with the membership never told these facts, ranks as betrayal of the worst kind. The solicitor sat by Lynk's elbow during the Council meeting and verbally challenged rulings from the chair. Democracy? They don't know the meaning of the word. If the membership realised how they were being manipulated, they couldn't possibly go along with them. But who's to tell them? The media certainly will not: there seems to be no way for us to get the message over.

Throughout the dispute, my feelings towards our Area leaders were not very complimentary. Roy Lynk and David Prendergast provoked feelings of hate and anger and their antics and attitudes will brand them as traitors to their class for all time – beyond even the boundaries set by the infamous George Spencer. To a trade unionist, it would be difficult to imagine a worse sin against the Labour movement.

Our other two leaders, Ray Chadburn and Henry Richardson, left me disappointed in their lack of open commitment to our cause. With Ray we never seemed to know whether he approved of what we were doing or not. Until he was actually removed by Lynk and co, he always gave me the impression he was more concerned with keeping his position; but to be perfectly fair to him, when he was put to the test by his opponents, he stuck by his principles and was sacked by them.

Henry was always willing to accommodate our needs whenever possible and I accept that he operated under exceptional difficulties, but his low profile throughout bothered me. That he would eventually be sacked through Lynk was never seriously in doubt, and I did make the point to him: 'Say publicly what you are saying to us privately.' Unfortunately it was quite a while before Henry could find a position within what was happening in the Notts coalfield. Instead of adopting his true position at the head of the strike organisation in the county, he always seemed to be outside it, which, given his true feelings, was a great pity.

Tuesday 15 January

Discussion at Ollerton mainly on power stations again: after Saturday's undertaking given to the T&G, the rota at West Burton was cocked up almost right away, with Sherwood failing their 8-hour commitment from 2–10pm. This is inviting withdrawal of virtually the only road support we have out there. Clipstone are to cover again for Sherwood this weekend and also for Thoresby at High Markham. Happily, at present our lads are prepared to do this; as things turned out, on getting back to Clipstone we also had to put a car on the road for a 4-hour cover, again for Sherwood from 2–6pm. John Brady seems to be having problems. Also discussed was the Notts situation relating to the scab union. The complaint among many lads is: 'Why should scabs be recruited back into the new Notts NUM when they have worked throughout?' This I can understand, but they have to realise this problem is quite apart from our main reason for being on strike. We cannot afford to refuse them membership if we are to smash Lynk's UDM[3] once and for all.

Wednesday 16 January
Plant pool rota, 7–9am, for me – it keeps snowing but will not freeze up.

Afters shift with numbers down, not surprising given the weather and other commitments. A few are also not now coming forward: one of them I visited this morning and was told he intends to keep his head down for the present. Two more talking of returning to work on Monday; one has been under a lot of pressure at home of late, but it's the other who will take him.

Thursday 17 January
Meeting at Ollerton at 7pm – a fair number of our lads and ladies made it. Richardson spoke reasonably well and put the cards on the table: we have to reorganise and we have to include scabs. Many were not very well-pleased about that, but on the whole his speech was well-received. An ASLEF lad then received a standing ovation for his history on their support for the strike and its effect on the movement of coal in this area. Following him was Chadburn, and I'm sorry to say he left us with a feeling of dismay: our people had gone there hoping to hear a rousing speech and encouragement to continue the fight, but

Coats out on picket line as weather deteriorates *(John Lowe)*

instead had to listen to his trials and tribulations. After the meeting our car-load stopped off at the Ollerton picket line; we expected a big crowd there following the meeting, but again there was a marked lack of commitment, with only a dozen or so bothering to stop. There was some verbal with the Essex police – we made them vacate their Transit to clear us from the pit lane end.

Friday 18 January

The central ladies' section are giving all groups £500 to buy coal for the lads. Even better news when our two lads in court at Retford returned: cases dismissed with £300 costs against the police. These two I was really concerned about – if found guilty, they could have been sent down. Their barrister TM has done a great job and we're grateful to him. McLachlan eat your heart out!

Our friend Chad phoned this evening. He was a little worried about us, with what's happening at present in Notts. I was able to reassure him that the fight was continuing but didn't tell him how hard our backs are being pressed against the wall.

Saturday 19 January

Learned mid-morning that the power station team 6am–2pm didn't go – the lad couldn't get the car started. At least he did ring the strike centre at Ollerton at 5.40am to inform them of the position. Hope they were able to cover; no doubt I'll get my bollocks chewed at Tuesday's meeting.

Sunday 20 January

Son-in-law today made a start on putting together possibly a book based on my diary throughout the dispute; don't know how it will turn out, but he seems confident. More power to his elbow; there's going to be a hell of a lot of this coming from this dispute and much of it is going to be in our favour.

Monday 21 January

Nationally, men are returning to work and this is very sad. They are not going back because the cause is wrong; after all this time the poor buggers are being forced back by all sorts of reasons: debt, a lack of money, food and fuel, and domestic and personal problems – these all play a part. Two of ours lost this week.

By the middle of January, we had lost a further four back to work, with still more seeming to be at risk. Surprisingly, we lived with this knowledge and were still able to remain cheerful – there was almost always laughter and horseplay among those using the centre. A strong feature of our relationships was that if a man decided he was going back to work, he did not creep back. Most of those who returned in the later stages made their position clear and at least I had a chance to discuss with many of them the reason for their decision to return; once a man had made up his mind, however, there was very little chance of him changing it – such decisions were made after much soul-searching.

Tuesday 22 January

Rent-a-mob this week are from Merseyside: although I don't recognise faces amongst them, it's the same strain from the same sty that gave us so much hassle three weeks ago. When we arrived at the pit for the day shift, they were still in the 'rest room' with two card schools going – our job then was to get them outside. If they're getting paid then they should earn it.

Power station rotas seemed to have been tightened with just a couple of instances of failure. The Markham cover checking on the other two has worked well. After the picket payout – which will unfortunately have to be a little less from next week – it was on to Chesterfield for the meeting to reorganise the Area Union. It started at 2pm and did not finish until 5.30pm. There are too many men attending: with twenty-five pits and three men from each, it makes for a rather unwieldy set-up. Talk of recruiting back en-bloc by branches led to fears of the strong possibility of scab officials being able to creep back in to continue their backstabbing work. A steering committee was also set up to coordinate the reorganisation of the new Area: these lads are to be fully committed and unavailable to take further part in the dispute. Weekly meetings will take place for the foreseeable future at the miners' offices at Chesterfield – and at least until branches have been formed. Of course all this assumes that the expulsion of Notts will take place, something not yet certain. How about these as slogans for our campaign: 'Sink Lynk' and 'We'll take away your breakaway'. Meanwhile Kinnock continues to embarrass us: in Westminster today he crossed swords with Maggie again but doesn't ever say the things we would expect of him if he were a true supporter. If only he accepted the feeling at the grass roots of the Labour Party and worked on that, we may just find the support we need.

Wednesday 23 January

Phone call this morning: a Bilsthorpe lad using our centre will be going back on Monday. He has family problems, with his son at college needing support. Hopefully this will be solved for him tomorrow through Henry Richardson's secretary PE – she's a gem.

Long-overdue meeting with the lads after dinner to bring them up to speed on every-thing: report on last night's meeting received better than I expected, with no objections. The need to get our case across at Sunday's branch meeting was accepted by all. The recruit back starts in the morning and leaflets will be available for then. The signs seem to be that we will have a good initial response. I'm setting no targets as yet, but I'll be disappointed if we don't get 200 very quickly. Area-wise, if we could get 5,000 in the first two-to-three weeks then Lynk would be in trouble. This would mean cash would be diverted from the scabs to the new Notts Division. Imagine: this new Area being financed by scabs in the midst of a major dispute.

Thursday 24 January

What a way to celebrate a wedding anniversary: thirty-two years wed today and I was at the pit by 5am – crazy days. Nine of us were in position and distributing leaflets by five-past; in no time there were more police around than we ever thought we were worth. And Channel 4 suddenly had a camera crew on the scene: their tactics were to swoop in whenever a bus arrived then hurry back across the road to the medical centre to catch

John and Elsie Lowe in younger times *(John Lowe)*

those walking in. There was no trouble, much to their dismay, while almost 600 leaflets were offered and accepted. By 6am those bastard Merseysiders had arrested one of the lads; I wasn't present at the time, but within minutes I was asking the sergeant for the reason. His reply: 'For being a smart arse.' It seems B Howkins made a comment to some lads going into work who refused to accept leaflets. The police ignored it, as the camera crew was present. When they got fed up and made to leave, B said: 'Don't go yet or they'll arrest us.' The sergeant poked his finger into B's face with the promise he would wipe the smile off it – only he put it a little more descriptively. When I called, Mansfield police station were no help whatsoever and told me to ring back at dinnertime. Legal centre informed and they took the matter in hand, but had no help in finding out the police's intentions either. B was released at 10.30am; what a waste of everyone's time and effort. He wasn't charged, just told he'd be cautioned.

Following the afters picket, we must have distributed 900 leaflets and believe most will be read; the first return came within minutes. Two of our lads reported something from Mansfield this afternoon I would love to be able to prove. In a quiet back street near the dole office they came across a large convoy of Transit vans, covered in mesh and unmarked. One of our lads spoke to someone standing close by as he took out a camera to take a shot; at that, all hell broke loose and he was chased by what he called 'gorillas in uniform', wielding pickaxe handles. He managed to get away and hide, but was badly shaken. Our suspicion is that men are being taken from the dole office to be bussed through the picket lines, thereby trying to convince our lads of the mass return. As yet, we have not decided what we can do about it. Discussion on the phone is out of the question as tonight there were noises as if someone was tuning in.

OUR UNION IS IN DANGER

PROPOSED RULE CHANGES COULD RESULT IN THE NOTTINGHAMSHIRE AREA BREAKING AWAY
FROM THE NATIONAL UNION OF MINEWORKERS

DON'T LET IT HAPPEN

ANTI-TRADE UNIONISTS MASTERMINDING THE PROPOSED CHANGES KNOW THAT WORKERS AND
STRIKERS ALIKE WILL NOT ALLOW THIS TO HAPPEN IF IT IS DONE OUT IN THE OPEN. VERY
EXPENSIVE LEGAL ADVICE HAS BEEN SOUGHT IN ORDER TO ACHIEVE THEIR AIMS BY BACK
DOOR METHODS.

DON'T LET THEM SUCCEED

BY GERRYMANDERING THE RULE BOOK THESE PEOPLE HOPE TO TAKE THE NOTTINGHAMSHIRE
AREA AWAY FROM THE AUTHORITY OF THE NATIONAL UNION AND RESURRECT SPENCERISM
IN THE NOTTINGHAMSHIRE COALFIELD.

DON'T LET THEM DO IT

BY ADDING CERTAIN WORDS, DELETING OR SUBSTITUTING OTHER WORDS, THE WHOLE
MEANING, CONTENT AND SPIRIT OF THE NOTTINGHAMSHIRE AREA RULE BOOK IS CHANGED.
THIS IS A MAJOR CHANGE OF OUR WHOLE CONSTITUTION. THE COMPLETE DETETION OF RULE
30 CAN NOT BE INTERPRETED IN ANY OTHER WAY THAN AS A BREAKAWAY FROM THE NATIONAL
UNION OF MINEWORKERS.

REMEMBER THE NOTTS. AREA MOTTO:

UNITY IS STRENGTH

FOR UNITED WE STAND - DIVIDED WE FALL

Information leaflet criticising rule changes *(John Lowe)*

I started this long day's report with the word 'crazy'; and it finishes that way also. At 1.20am one of the lads who has been away fundraising was knocking on my door: he has thought so deeply on the shortcomings of our overall strategy, he has devised his own plans – and felt it necessary to travel from Grimsby to my house to tell me of them immediately. Like the bloody idiot I am, I sat and talked with him until 4.10am. He's a good lad, enthusiastic, but the realities of our position and the restriction we face, plus his continued absence from the picket line, all served to restrict his understanding of certain basic facts.

The case of the Transits in Mansfield was one we decided to follow up after talking the problem through with Jimmy Hood, who agreed to make some funding available to mount a surveillance operation. We set cars to watch the exit roads from Mansfield: our initial findings were a 'scab van' picking up in Pleasley and going on towards Clowne, and police patrol cars patrolling the supposedly closed office block near the dole office, which showed signs of activity with many lights on inside and three wire-mesh Transits still in the closed-off yard. We then found that the vans were certainly driving into Yorkshire and taking part in the 'scab runs' there, with police escorts all the way – but that Notts men were not taking part. What surprised us was that the drivers were Yorkshiremen, some of them from the pit villages they were driving to: I was very saddened to think that such treachery could be enacted by working class people against what were, perhaps, members of their own families. We learnt this by sending two lads disguised as Electricity Board workers into the café where they met upon their return to Mansfield; the photographer we positioned across the road was spotted and chased by the drivers then, backed up with four of our biggest lads, his second attempt also proved unsuccessful due to the volume of traffic. We passed on our find to interested parties, but thereafter the police must have found new premises from which to operate.

The tactics quite deliberately used by the Government to undermine and demoralise our membership were also in evidence that week. Peter Heathfield, NUM general secretary, and NCB's industrial relations officer Ned Smith seemed to have found a basis for negotiation without preconditions – then in went the establishment boot once more, with MacGregor demanding a signed statement of our position before sanctioning any resumption of talks. The situation had been widely reported for days, building hope among a great many people that an honourable settlement could be reached; then again we saw the final execution of that cruel ploy – raise expectations then deliberately dash them. Brutal, but undoubtedly effective.

Friday 25 January

Not only was I knackered with last night's experience but my wife also had no sleep – to say she was in an ugly mood is to put it mildly. No day shift picket for me. Little response so far from the leaflets; we did expect a few back today, but on reflection Sunday, after the meeting, and Monday is a more realistic prospect.

Saturday 26 January

Four Welsh Executive members and representatives of their ladies' section at the Ollerton meeting – their main aim is to build and consolidate bridges between all Areas. A suggestion of twinning between pits and centres was made. Reassurance of their support for the need to expel Notts was given; however, they said their priority is foremost the strike and efforts to find a solution and secondly the expulsion. I see the position differently: the unconstitutional actions of Notts are a bushfire which, if not tackled immediately, could get out of hand. Once control of the situation is lost, the task of rebuilding will take many years – during which time the Board could do as it likes. Large-scale support has already been promised: Lynk must be running scared. Talks with the Board are due to start on Tuesday next; our Welsh friends assure us there will be no sell-out. I hope they're bloody right.

Sunday 27 January

Our follow-up leaflet on the proposed NUM Notts Division handed out to the men going into the branch meeting; only a few refused them and hopefully most will read it. Inside the meeting there wasn't much sign they had, with the usual noisy nine-day week men much in evidence. This we expect, but had hoped for a bigger turnout; only 200 estimated against my hope for 600–700. Ray Chadburn, agent for Clipstone as well as Area president, was at the meeting; his presence was resented by a number of our Tory opposites. He spoke for approximately forty-five minutes and was interrupted a number of times, notably by M's sarcasm and ridicule. Ray made a number of telling points, however, such as the vulnerability of Notts if the expulsion comes – he promised his resignation if Notts persists in going it alone and reminded them of our beginnings as a national union and of the black days of Spencerism. M's reply took quite some time and contained the usual hypocrisy: that he'd voted for strike, voted for Scargill, supported the Welsh miners in 1981, etc. Then his hobby horse: democracy. Chadburn told him 'democracy' is the most prostituted word in the English language and that it has been used and ignored by Notts as and when it suits them; he highlighted the example of 1977 and the National ballot on the incentive scheme, when the Area went to court against a ballot result. It didn't give a damn about democracy then.

Monday 28 January

The new lot from Hampshire left us alone – as long as they keep away from our shoulders, I don't mind. How times have changed! At one time, I expected to talk with their senior officer; indeed, they came out to talk with me. In this way, we avoided a lot of potential trouble.

Nationally, the media is preaching the end for us; Chadburn and Scargill were given a chance tonight on TV for a change and both spoke well. What cheered me was the bank rate being raised, the struggle over oil prices and particularly the nosedive of the share price index. At one point it had fallen forty-five points, and finished the day twenty-five down. Maggie's friends won't stand much of this, I'm happy to forecast.

Tuesday 29 January

Picket managers' meeting – our friend in the T&G has warned that his tankers are getting through but we are not reporting it. If we are not there to do so, he will have to remove his support. Three Shirebrook lads at the meeting wanting to get involved with us; although we are aware of the cash restraints, I feel it's a sad reflection on their strike leaders if they are not keeping them occupied. They were advised to go to Shireoaks or Manton picket lines whenever possible.

Wednesday 30 January
Just a token picket now: as long as we have a presence, the scabs have to cross an OFFICIAL PICKET LINE. The lads are responding well with both the picket and the watches on roads and facilities we've been conducting recently; few meaningful results from the latter as yet, but if our suspicions are confirmed the evidence will prove useful when the time comes. It won't do us much good in the short-term, though. Yesterday we had two cars of flyers out at Shireoaks and the deputies turned back – job done and the lads came home. Petrol money well-spent.

The NCB is maintaining its hard line, demanding a guarantee that pit closures be considered; Union this afternoon talking with TUC in a bid to get the Board to the table. We are now to switch our watch to the next junction down the motorway; a watch on the yard base will be made from late tonight until 3am because by 3.30am this morning the yard was empty, meaning we had missed whatever activity there had been. We knew we needed patience and so it proves: we haven't yet found the picking-up point or the times they start. My limited cash float is being eaten away – tomorrow I'll have to convince the powers-that-be to back me further. Scare stories inside the pit are still being put about – seems they're being told if they join us by signing our leaflet then they'll lose their Notts pension rights. Untrue. The time is long overdue for personalising the issue: the characters of so many of these so-called leaders leave much to be desired and yet we continue to fight clean. Why?

Thursday 31 January
Pains in the chest and short of breath; getting no better and I'm anxious about it persisting.

Afternoon meeting at Chesterfield meant I missed an announcement by the ladies which has upset many of us: they cannot afford to fund the expenses of the Land Rover and the saw. If they did it would mean a cut in the food parcels. This really is ridiculous: £25 to be able to get coal and logs out to the lads is a small price to pay. I hope they are not developing a bank book mentality. The meeting – the crippling decision to postpone the delegate conference, although unavoidable, means the initiative has been lost: until the expulsion is a reality, we have an uphill battle in front of us. Cash is a problem: our steering committee cannot produce the propaganda we need to back us at pit level. The one leaflet we have distributed so far – produced by National – has resulted in Lynk threatening to take it to court.

Tonight I became a grandfather again. Our latest little girl weighs in at 7lb; she's now no. 8 in line of succession for the John Lowe fortune. She's a little cracker – Grandma and myself have another anxiety eased as mother and daughter are doing well.

Friday 1 February
The police are definitely using the softly-softly approach again. Doesn't wash – the Thoresby lads saw their picket manager arrested yesterday. Although the number of arrests has drastically reduced, they are still prepared to let us know they are there at

certain times, and we can never trust them. Revelation that the 'scab van' drivers are Yorkshiremen: the sort of comment overheard by our spies was 'If they had my picture back in my village, I'm as good as dead' and 'Good job I had my mask on the other day – my mate was stood at the front of the picket line'. They talked of the Kiveton run, saying the pit will probably be back on three-shifts in a couple of weeks. With animals like these prepared to sell their own class, even their own neighbours, and possibly even their own families, one despairs.

Saturday 2 February
Social evening tonight should be a good show: 200 tickets sold. Henry Richardson said he hoped to be there and an invitation to Scargill has also been sent. What a lift for the lads and their wives if some of these people made the effort to get round our Notts centres.

Sunday 3 February
Last night was fantastic – quite a lot came from other centres and the place was solid. By the end of the evening we were stood on tables and chairs, hands linked and singing our heads off. They were still dancing when I left at midnight – hope there aren't too many complaints about the noise. Bevercotes with power station problems this morning – called at 8.45am for a car to cover their Cottam rota, 10am–2pm. I could only raise D Broadfoot and his car. He's gone to take one lad away from our lot at West Burton to cover with him; appreciate that, D.

Monday 4 February
Hampshire police outnumbered us two-to-one at day shift. There could be trouble with their inspector before the week is out: he was demanding names and colliery check numbers of everyone. When I refused, a confrontation blew up: he didn't like being challenged and questioned back on his knowledge of the law. Two cars and eight men were at Kiveton by 4.30am. Expecting a mass picket, they found only Notts lads there, approx seventy. That no Yorkshiremen were present to picket their own scabs is a disturbing thought: if this is indicative of their frame of mind, the fight is as good as over. The only satisfaction for our lads was when they were able to give it some 'Yorkshire scabs' to those going in for a change. Scargill and Jack Taylor on breakfast TV this morning: I have to say I detected a note of finality – resignation, perhaps – in Taylor's speaking. He should be out in his Area, encouraging his lads. Leading from the bloody front seems to have been forgotten of late; in our case, it never even got off the ground.

Afternoon picket we were joined by friends from London – almost thirty pickets for a change. With weather like this, we'll soon be bloody sunbathing again. Propaganda machine keeps turning it out: figures for the 'flood back' today means by now there should be 110 per cent of the original workforce back.

Tonight Ned Smith was interviewed on Channel 4 – he's now taken retirement from his job as head of industrial relations with the Board. His message to us was that the strike is lost, obviously. He was also saying that the Board should soften its attitude and negotiate a settlement to get us back with dignity. Bullshit. If the man had any bottle, he'd come out and give the true reasons for his leaving: that the Board is in disarray thanks to the 'hawks'; that he has serious differences with the likes of MacGregor; that direct access to No. 10 has been the order of the day.

Tuesday 5 February

There is much dissatisfaction with the seeming lack of concern by National leaders over our position in Notts and at the lack of information given us: we only found out by phoning HQ in Sheffield that the National Executive meeting has been put back to next Thursday. They don't seem to place importance on the expulsion issue and we suspect that suspension is in some minds as an alternative; if this were to happen, our lads would leave us in double-quick time. Lynk is telling the scabs that Notts will not be expelled; they are sitting on the fence instead of returning our forms.

Flyers for the rest of the week at two per day sorted out, with the Kiveton day shift again the target; there could be something like forty cars travelling. It was felt at the picket managers' meeting that the propaganda of Notts men into Yorkshire was worth the cost – I expect some difficulties getting through roadblocks as police activity intensifies. At Shireoaks, where lads have been getting through without much trouble, the roadblocks have now been widened and the lads find they have to park up and walk the last mile or so to picket the deputies. Collection in Nottingham: two volunteers for Thursday despite it not being our turn. I don't like having to do this, but if others persist, so must we.

This decision was a sure sign of our financial desperation. There were some other pits that had consistently gone out of turn and now, I'm ashamed to admit, here I was adding to the chaos. Worse, I had reached the stage where I did not care: the need for cash to sustain our transport was great while our means for acquiring it were limited.

That the strike was now slowly crumbling I could no longer deny. My hope for some time past had been that the cost to the Government would be so great that common sense would finally enter the equation; also that fellow trade unionists, seeing how we were being crucified, would offer help in bringing the matter to a head. Sadly, neither was to be.

With the benefit of hindsight, I never cease to marvel at the way we coped as a group. We picketed at one end of what was a long, sprawling village; our single strike telephone was at the opposite end; and in the centre of the village was our strike centre/soup kitchen which was the focal point for most, where activities were organised. Very often I felt I was astride two great chasms while needing to be in half a dozen places at once. We were a well-fed and close-knit group whose morale was surprisingly high, but the mental and emotional pressures were now intolerable.

Wednesday 6 February

Executive meeting in Sheffield is now back on for tomorrow. The media are putting out the story that the South Wales Area is to ask for a return to work without agreement. So many things need considering before such a move is even suggested: with over 600 lads sacked, their future is of prime importance – pledges have been made that must be kept – while the closure programme could be applied without any serious opposition. The position of many of the Notts lads is also very precarious: at many pits, branch officials and workmen have openly stated that they don't want strikers back and will not work with them. In addition to all of this, we have no guarantee that the Notts expulsion will even be on the agenda – we in Notts could really be on Shit Street.

From my brother-in-law tonight: his Crown Court trial at Derby on trumped-up charges is going badly this first day. End of today's report before I really spoil my manners.

Thursday 7 February

Flyers to Kiveton were back by 6.15am. Not so many it seems made it, although if our lads didn't have any trouble more ought to have been there – the petrol money paid out on Tuesday should have guaranteed well over a 100-strong picket. If some of the cars promised have instead travelled to Sheffield this morning, discipline has once again fallen down. Told last night by Jim Dowen that the reported move by South Wales, still being put out today, will not even be on the agenda there.

John Lowe smoking cigarette in strike centre *(John Lowe)*

I'm afraid my movements are severely restricted at the moment; the more running around I do, the worse I get. Probably I'm also suffering from depression. It's not about losing heart – in this I'm a fighter and will only go back when our National leadership tell me to. Executive meeting broke up this afternoon with an announcement from both NACODS and the NUM to say the Board must get back to the table; if they refuse, they'll ask ACAS to conduct a public enquiry. I have no faith that this will happen. Great news: the charges against my brother-in-law have been dropped; in fact, the case was thrown out of court. Thank God.

Friday 8 February
The message from Sheffield is not very encouraging: unless we get back 3,000 slips for the new Notts Division, we don't look like getting support for it from National. How the bloody hell do they expect us to operate against Lynk's union when they won't reconvene the delegate conference with the threat of expulsion? They won't give us any financial backing and even seem reluctant to come into Notts to speak. Richardson tells us we have the support of the Executive, but everything we hear – which is not much – suggests otherwise.

On the news tonight it was announced that Mac the Knife is considering 'sacking' all strikers once the figure at work reaches over 50 per cent. This Yankee is following just the same procedure as when he broke the strike of the American miners. If NACODS now don't make a positive move, what does it take to get them angry?

Saturday 9 February
Weather very cold today with snow, ice and temperatures well below freezing point. Afraid the lads on power station cover this weekend have a most unenviable job: eight hours out there in this weather, without a fire or shelter, shows commitment of the highest order. Scab tankers – Total and now Wincanton – are going by the lads without a second glance. These Trent Valley stations are just as much at risk from nuclear power as we are from Mac's axe.

On the Sunday a group of us attended our first Labour Party meeting of the Forest Town group; by the end I felt physically sick at the performance of some of those present. The patronising attitude of superscab and branch chairman M – a councillor – made me feel very bitter while Don Concannon got me angry: he had recently been readopted by the constituency party and this visit was to thank the branch for their support. His anti-NUM stance throughout the dispute and Westminster comments in particular were designed for local consumption, without a principle in sight. We were to realise very quickly that before these people could be exposed as shallow, much more involvement from the activists would be needed. We learned at that meeting, for example, that the manifesto for the forthcoming county council elections was even then being treated with contempt – the same people who were altering our rule book as they saw fit were doing the same there.

Sunday 10 February

Sad to hear today of the death of Ernest Hackett, an old-time left-winger. Both Ernest and particularly Ida his wife have been a tower of strength behind the miners' support groups. We at Clipstone centre feel deeply for Ida at this time.

Monday 11 February

From early this morning we've had the biggest police operation in many months: road-blocks and countless officers both on foot and in Transit vans dispersed throughout the village. They must have been tapping the wrong phones because it looked as though they expected an influx of lads into Clipstone. We now have to face the fact that in Notts we are potential targets for revenge by the scabs: numerous minor outbreaks have occurred these last few months, but nothing of a lasting nature. In the last few days, however, there have been two instances of windows being broken. I say with certainty that this sort of action has never been a part of our campaign – even when cars have been vandalised, anger has never spilled over into like-for-like retaliation or violence.

An announcement tonight on TV attributed to Ken Sampey[4] to say they would not be going on strike, whatever happens. Although I personally expected nothing different, a lot of people have been hoping and praying for their involvement. Afraid Richardson looks like getting some stick on Thursday after his forecast at last Friday's meeting that the deputies would strike if the Board did not return to the table this week.

Tuesday 12 February

Picket managers' meeting: our power station picket discipline has apparently gone for a Burton, with gaps showing all week. Calling off the picket out there was raised, but just as quickly squashed. Five pits have mandated to lift the overtime ban, while two were against it; one other, we suspect, will vote to lift despite not having a mandate. This move has been pushed from Berry Hill.

Hardship cases now piling up at an alarming rate. One today is particularly serious, with the lad standing to lose his house in spite of what many would regard as a generous payment from the Area hardship fund. The fund will now only consider claims put through by the picket managers. This places an intolerable burden on one man; I'm not prepared to act as God. A sub-committee, with two of us and two from the ladies' section, to deal with our claims is to be formed – in this way some sort of order and discipline can be maintained. More injunctions today following those yesterday, when mass pickets at four Welsh pits were made illegal – those today involve eleven Yorkshire pits. These judgements and others from throughout this dispute will be used as yardsticks for years to come.

Wednesday 13 February

Spoke to a number of those going through the dinnertime picket about returning the leaflets. I think we can reasonably expect a few back yet if we work at it. The individual approach is the only way to do it: we've found that if we talk to them directly, particularly the younger ones, we can overcome their reluctance. At the afternoon strike meeting a full report on the present situation was given: we informed the lads of the new arrange-ments for hardship allowance and also asked for more commitment from some who were receiving picket money. No one seemed disturbed at the time, but I was later visited by two of them: they resented our views on picket money – note that both have been doing very little – while on the hardship they were against what they termed 'means-testing'. A third lad had also visited me by the evening to complain about the hardship system. Yorkshire Area today agreed to comply with the injunction on 'mass picketing'; the scabs' vocabulary seems limited to writ and injunction. It's going to take a long time to sort out the legal tangle that these traitors have laid on for us. The true cost of the strike is now coming out: the Electricity Generating Board losses for last year are going to show over £2 billion – staggering. With the pound going through the floor (dollar–pound parity imminent), the share price index falling (twenty-one points yesterday) and the police cost not even thought of yet, Nigel Lawson's Budget plans look sick.

Thursday 14 February
Funeral today of Ernest Hackett – three men and two women went along to show our respect and sympathy. Ida is an amazing woman – her strength and stamina is standing her in good stead in spite of her seventy years. Old Sid is not too good at present – the doctor has seen him today but we'll have to keep an eye on him. Loyalty like his must be remembered.

Friday 15 February
Very thin on the ground: only five lads bothered to turn out. I understand up to a point, but the supposed pep-talk on Wednesday has apparently not paid off. They are as sick as myself of standing and not seeming to achieve anything.

The prospect of talks seem brighter today: our Executive and NACODS have spent the full day in talks at the TUC with that body's general secretary Norman Willis. Little has been given out so far (at 8.30pm) but we need some light to keep the lads actively involved.

Later – seems that talks about talks will not now take place.

Saturday 16 February
Trip to Wellingborough. The flu bug has really had a go at us today: from the sixty-six names we had on the list, only fifty made it. One of those who dropped out was Mal Howarth, who was to be the NUM speaker. We arrived to a sparsely-attended meeting, but the main speaker Bob Cryer was well worth listening to. He not only touched on the miners' strike but on many other aspects of political and economic life today. My contribution was to enlighten the local supporters on the unenviable position of Notts strikers at this time in relation to the proposed expulsion and the strike. Without opportunity to prepare anything I was a little reluctant to speak; but if we could not talk from experience before, now is the time that we can. We were given a meal at a local pub and entertained by a folk group. Everyone finished the night in great style: they were able to listen to and sing strike songs they'd never heard before.

Monday 18 February
Worst morning yet. Only two at the pit for the day shift picket – seems like morale has reached rock-bottom. Clipstone welfare have presented us with three electricity bills totalling £1,013; having already asked the Clipstone Branch and Notts Area to pay,

they are now suggesting we try National. They are not yet threatening to cut us off. The injunction we served on Notts Area to stop the rules changes going through will be taken up again shortly. I've now reached the stage where I want the rule changes to stand: this, coupled with the potential lifting of the overtime ban, should be enough to guarantee the Notts expulsion. The ballot to lift the overtime ban at Clipstone resulted in 900 votes with a two-to-one majority in favour.

Tuesday 19 February
The flu bug really has hold of me and I feel washed out; told later that only two at the pit this morning. Two cars, eight lads away to Shireoaks and deputies turned back again. They really are a NACODS branch with courage, unlike most of their colleagues; Dinnington also turn back, but not Kiveton.

The big rally in London on Sunday: we have seven seats allotted to us and these will be drawn out tomorrow. For myself, I have no interest; I'm feeling low and would be better off away from the lads for a while. Lads told we're to start paying out money on pickets done from next week: we are looking for improved support from most, but from a small section in particular – one lad has been nowhere near the picket line for weeks and is making noises that he'll go back to work if his money is stopped. So be it. I'll not be blackmailed; when one gets away with everything the rot sets in elsewhere, as seen these last two mornings.

Wednesday 20 February
An improvement on picketing numbers: six for the day shift and thirty for the afters, added to eight flyers and two breakfast staff plus the logging team – gives us a result almost 100 per cent up on certain days recently. Recruit back boosted when seven were handed in by one who went back – this now brings us to over 100. If others followed our tactics, distasteful as they are, many more could be signed up throughout the Area.

TUC plugging away: Norman Willis saw Energy Secretary Peter Walker last night and was supposed to report back to our Executive this morning. He instead went to see the Board; as of 6pm the Executive and Sampey are convened to listen to what Willis has to report. The lads are afraid of a sell-out; we have to keep telling them otherwise and try to believe it. There are so many points to resolve: after reaching a basis for some sort of agreement on the pit closure programme, there has to be an amnesty for nearly 700 who have been sacked. This could prove a sticking point: we've never been faced with this level in previous disputes. The 5.2 per cent wage increase already implemented by scabby Notts for 1983–84 has to be sorted plus the 1984–85 round of negotiations which haven't yet been put due to the dispute.

Latest tonight is that the revised offer obtained by the TUC from the Board was described by our Executive members as worse than the last one; accordingly, it was turned down by the full Executive. More pressure is needed from other quarters and it has to be maintained. The cost of the whole operation has to be made prohibitive to both the Board and Maggie. This can still be achieved: with the Budget due shortly, it is now accountancy time. However it is obvious that she is prepared to take us to bankruptcy; brinkmanship has become the name of the game.

Thursday 21 February

Afraid I've been out of the fight. Wrong to say I'm disillusioned – my biggest problem is this bug. No reports from the flyers or picket line – I suppose if anything had happened, I would have been told. Internationally Maggie continues to court Regan. Her efforts while in America have been nothing short of obscene.

Friday 22 February

Maggie comes home! What a kick in the teeth for her. She'd not set foot before Regan was telling the European countries what they must do to catch up with the American economy. What a bloody laugh. He's cutting investment across the board – except for the arms race, or, as he puts it, defence spending. Our delegate conference yesterday came out over-whelmingly against the Board's demands: after all the shit printed about Scargill – and 'if the full Executive were involved' etc – the fact that not only the Executive but the full delegate conference has rejected the Board has been totally ignored by the media.

Our Feb *Strike Back* edition is now ready for being put out, thanks to the efforts of retired Coal Board employee JB. A remarkable lady: she makes regular donations to women's support groups, spends hours at the legal centre engaged in shorthand and typing sessions, and is instrumental to the news sheet and many leaflets we have put out – all the more remarkable considering the physical disabilities she operates under. *Strike Back* has gone from strength to strength: we now even have, surprisingly, a demand from Yorkshire. It's now read from Whitby across to Pendle, down in Brighton and into London. Do we get about! We may have to publish the full range of our issues, six plus two special editions: perhaps we should send them to Prince Philip after he spoke out today saying the people in work should get recognition rather than people on the dole – he should have learned by now to keep his mouth shut on things he knows nothing about. Maybe he was speaking about scabby Notts without actually daring to say so.

Saturday 23 February

Used the last of our coal today. We've been lucky right through, managing to get the odd bag given and burning it sparingly with logs; our good neighbour has helped out us and others and we owe him gratitude. The kids on holiday in Belgium are due home this evening; another set are due to go to France shortly and at Easter yet another lot go to Amsterdam. We must never forget our brothers over the Channel.

The Board are offering an immediate advance of £100 to those returning now. How bloody corrupt are they prepared to be.

Sunday 24 February

Didn't attend the branch meeting because of my revulsion for the so-called leadership – both official and unofficial – at Clipstone, who dominate the meetings. I hope that the need to attend will not be with us for much longer and the expulsion will be fact. Power station lads reported back this afternoon that twenty-two tankers went through. No coal moving in but coal-burn inside this morning. Usually at the weekend it's chiefly oil-burn till mid-afternoon, but it would seem they are desperately short of oil at present.

STRIKE BACK CLIPSTONE

ISSUE NO. 6.   February 1985.

As March approaches, so we come to the first
anniversary of this most damaging dispute. It would
seem timely to remind the "Working Notts. Miners"
of their responsibility for its prolongation. That
they allowed themselves to be led down the road to
shame by so-called leaders who are without scruple,
will be no excuse when the history of this period
is written.

The principle and commitment shown by the real heroes
of Notts. should serve to shame all those who have
worked against the National Union and the fight for
jobs and communities.

When future generations ask "What did you do in the
strike" what will their answer be?

Our answer will be "Better to die on our feet than
live in shame on our knees!"

DATE to remember:

Sat. March 2nd – Coachload of supporters from
   2 o'clock   Pendle will arrive at St. John's
                  Hut. Dinner will be prepared for
                  them.
                  Evening at Community Centre to follow.

         Let's give them a warm welcome – a full turnout.

Issue number six of *Strike Back* (John Lowe)

The London demo: the early evening news showed big trouble in Whitehall. One of our lads, D Carmody, seen on TV being taken away after sitting in the road; I immediately made contact with London after it was announced fifty arrests had been made. The contact promised to call back by 10pm after checking with the three 'nicks' being used for holding the lads. As yet, at 10.30pm, no word has come. I've received a call from one of the lads who made it back, one of three who had to jump on the Blidworth bus – they got separated from their four mates. His account seems very much like the previous experience: arrests in the middle of the column which prompted the second half to halt until the lads were brought back. This time the police were ready, sealing off both ends of the street and moving in force. Horses were seen on TV charging amongst the crowd, with women and children visible. Police on foot in huge numbers went in and we saw their boots going in; how the hell the public can be prepared to put up with the style of policing we now have completely mystifies me. One of our lads came to see me tonight to say he may be starting back this week: another typical case of pressure from bills mounting, marital problems and no light at the end of the tunnel. It is quite a legitimate complaint. After a lengthy talk he went away to consider what we talked of; I'm hoping to see him again tomorrow to see what we can work out – but yes, I've got my fingers crossed.

Told at 11.15pm that two more of the lads are back, while a call from London to say that the others cannot be identified at the 'nicks'; M has had a busy night, ferrying lads about London after they were released on police bail. He's a good lad.

Our Notts strike fund was paying the cost of sending two cars per group into Yorkshire. I was at a loss to understand why, with so many men on strike in the Yorkshire coalfield, they needed to rely on our efforts to picket out their deputies; it seemed to me that when faced with the kind of situation we had endured throughout, too many of their men just bottled out. I suggested to a picket managers' meeting that we should start targeting pits in the Notts Area once more, pointing out that I could send twice the number of cars locally at no extra cost to ourselves. The lads got a lift out of the local operation and were desperate to get on the road, but I was in a minority and lost the argument.

Another chief concern that ate up time was benefits: in February the processing of our claims had been transferred to the Chesterfield office of the DHSS with all queries to be directed there; the line seemed continually engaged and it was often the same situation with child benefit in Newcastle. On one particular day I tried to raise social services in Mansfield instead, but was informed the person I wanted was not available; the next day I desperately tried to contact the regional office of the DHSS in Birmingham, again a failure. I decided then to go to the top – the head office in London. Bingo! I must have ruffled a few feathers as the day after everything was resolved with them, I received a message from Chesterfield from someone who appeared to have been mauled by their London superiors: I was told that I could have almost instant service whenever needed, but 'please don't repeat the performance with London again'.

Monday 25 February

Marathon phone session again trying to get Newcastle re: child benefit, NUPE in Nottingham and veg wholesaler re: delivery of bad spuds. A similar session this afternoon got me two out of three. Had to knock off afternoon picket to take a case of hardship to Mansfield – could have been done by someone else but was asked by the lad himself in preference to his own picket manager. One of the two lads left in London was arrested and held overnight; both are okay.

The numbers game goes on and the claims now, if true, would mark the beginning of the end. Today they are claiming over 3,000; the difference between the Board and Union's figures differ by something like fifteen per cent. We haven't lost anyone further as of yet.

Tuesday 26 February

Good feeling this morning with ten at the pit plus the flyers and kitchen staff. Notts rent-a-mob seem to be with us this week and doing their best to ignore us. The scabs try to act as if we are not there when passing and we have long since run out of things to shout; it's probably best, politically, not to be too abusive in view of the possible recruit back and 'smash Lynk' campaign.

Upset this afternoon when we lost the lad we were expecting to go back: I cannot criticise him knowing what he has done for us in the past and the pressures he's been under. Decided we would levy the lads 50p for the next two weeks in aid of the French mining disaster: this has so far claimed twenty-two lives with 105 injured. The thoughts and sympathy of many will be with them at this time.

There has been a move by certain people for a vote on an organised return to work – the unanimous decision of the strike committee is to reject any idea along those lines; further-more, we will not even allow a discussion on the subject at tomorrow's full strike meeting.

Wednesday 27 February

Ollerton's Mick McGinty in attendance at the meeting along with a comrade from Australia who is a shop steward in a brewery out there. Among the items discussed was the proposed rally and demonstration at Ollerton to mark the anniversary of Davey Jones, the Yorkshire lad who died of injuries sustained there. To be held on 15 March, it will be well-supported. Mick gave us an account of his fundraising trip to America – it sounded worthwhile but we can't be sure until the promises made become cash. A good meeting: if we lose any more this week, it will be because they have already made up their minds.

An alarming call this afternoon from Area strike HQ to say a special meeting tomorrow at Warsop Main to decide whether or not to return. If this happens at one pit, it could easily spread. We must lobby and stress that those sacked will be left without a chance. Morale raised a little when son-in-law who is scabbing at nearby Mansfield Colliery called to ask if I could supply him with some recruiting forms. He's asking for a dozen – he can have them with pleasure. Board now claiming 50 per cent back at work – Maggie says it's good news.

Two more stories of police impartiality. Mick's wife received threatening phone calls from an individual and so he stopped the person concerned and, in words often used, said: 'Phone my wife again, lad, and I'll kill you.' Complaints to the police led to him being charged with threatening behaviour and threatening to kill. In normal circumstances, Mick's wife would be the injured party and the scab the one in trouble; now Mick faces charges that carry penalties of up to ten years in jail – or so he's been advised. The second one involves a pensioner at Sherwood who was involved in an argument with a scab. The pensioner wears a calliper on one arm and is pushing seventy. The police have seen fit to charge him with ABH.

Thursday 28 February
Still a hell of a lot of scabs will not meet our gaze. I wonder why, after all this time? More success for the flyers; the story goes that while the Notts lads are limiting the production of coal, those in Yorkshire are busy fundraising. Three cars arranged for tomorrow and for a change I'm going with them; suppose I could, even should, have been away more. Three cars away too to lobby the Warsop meeting; they were not needed as a return was not even under discussion – rather it was discussed in a National context and they agreed they will return only when instructed.

A special delegate conference has been called for Sunday. Letters and statements from the Board show that their intention is one of total surrender on our part. I'm prepared to fight the bastards till the end, but how much further we can expect the lads to go is difficult to see at present. The Notts expulsion is very unlikely to be on the agenda – in fact it's possible that it won't be discussed until after the dispute. NACODS meeting today: Midland Area decided they would not supervise overtime in the Notts Area. What a bloody laugh – is it supposed to be some big deal? These management mice could have been a deciding factor long ago. They've stood by and seen us hammered from all sides and not lifted a finger to help. Trade unionists?

Notes
1. He served time in jail for this
2. Police Support Unit
3. Union of Democratic Mineworkers – formerly the National Working Miners' Committee, mentioned previously
4. NACODS president

PART FIVE

MARCH 1985–

Friday 1 March

A disturbing phone call last night from Jim Dowen after he talked with Henry Richardson about yesterday's National Executive meeting: I'm afraid all the signs point to us losing the battle over the weekend. Some Areas are advocating an 'orderly return without agreement' next week – if this happens, our position in Notts is very precarious.

> This was now the final run-in of the great pit strike for jobs, with several Areas seemingly favouring a return without agreement. Throughout the coalfields, Area delegate conferences would take place on the Saturday to mandate their delegates for the national conference the following day; an air of inevitability settled on every-one and comments such as 'it's only the first round' and 'one lost battle does not lose the war' were expressed all around. There was no shortage of defiance from both the lads and our womenfolk: I recorded at the time that my admiration for them had reached even greater heights.
>
> Anger and frustration had not yet given way to the reality of a return and the sadness that would bring; even so, the fight was not yet over.

Friday 1 March (continued)

The deputies at Shireoaks turned back thanks to a picket of around seventy men; at Dinnington, also, they turned. This morning we've been asked to lobby a meeting at Shirebrook miners welfare; only been able to get two cars, but I'll be going with them again. A measure of their dedication is that one of the cars will be going on from the lobby to meet the Shirebrook railmen ASLEF branch; this has become a regular Friday practice and even now the lads are keen to keep the rail support to the last.

The lobby – almost no response from other branches with six Clipstone, one Mansfield and one Warsop bothering to go. Result of the meeting was a decision to go with the conference decision on Sunday.

This afternoon I had a phone call to say 'call off the power station picket'; the bloody bottom fell out of my world. The unthinkable now looks like becoming reality. As I write now I'm angry; I feel very emotional, betrayed, sold out; and very, very sad. There is nothing the National leadership can do about it, I know. We've been betrayed by the rest of the trade union movement, with certain exceptions. They'll rue the day they turned their backs on us. My anger is also directed at South Wales, who we see as responsible for planting the idea of return without settlement. Since they raised it weeks ago, I know the drift back to work has accelerated.

I felt bitterness towards Bill Sirs, the leader of the steelmen's union. He it was who told Scargill: 'Don't let them do to your industry, Arthur, what they have done to mine.' After urging us to resist MacGregor, the butcher of his own union, he then turned his back on any cooperation with our cause.

Ken Sampey and Peter McNestry, the leaders of NACODS, will bear my undying contempt for their sell-out, not only of my union, but of the future of their own members also. When they were faced with a situation where they had to 'put up or shut up', they tamely bottled out.

Neil Kinnock and many senior members of the Labour Party leadership will long be remembered for the way they turned their backs on us in spite of the over-whelming evidence of the conspiracy being practised against us.

Many other leaders of influential unions ducked their heads below the battlements rather than be seen to be supporting us; although many of them would deny it, history will show how little they cared while Thatcher beat us into submission.

Perhaps worst of all were the attitudes of Eric Hammond of the electrical trade union and Gavin Laird and Bill Jordan of the engineers. They should be exposed as willing tools of Thatcherism. The struggles of our forefathers count for so very little it seems, now that the 'me now' mentality has become accepted as the norm.

Friday 1 March (continued)
The programme on the miners' strike tonight came over not quite as I'd expected. David Dimbleby, joined by Eaton and Scargill in the Birmingham studio, if anything favoured Arthur. Eaton came over as his usual bumbling self – he offered no hope whatsoever for a settlement, insisting that the document presented by Willis to our side was a TUC/NCB document. The lie to this is well-documented and Willis, although lying low, has not supported the Board. The scabs at Cotgrave were easily put down by Scargill.

Saturday 2 March
The media have already decided that a majority of delegates will vote tomorrow for a return to work. If the conference decides to carry on the strike, we will lose a number of our lads anyway. It's heartbreaking to think it but they've taken so many knocks, hopes repeatedly raised and dashed, that they're at the end of their tether; that doesn't mean though that they aren't angry and disillusioned at the outcome, while they're sick at the thought of the 700 sacked men out in the cold. A few I wouldn't expect to get their jobs

back, but if there's any natural justice the overwhelming majority would be reinstated; I say further that the fact that they were dismissed in the first place should shame the Board for punishing twice what in most cases were fit-ups.

When questioned on the possibility of a return, I would only say that as far as I was concerned speculation was not an option and like any good soldier, I would only follow the last order. Unless we heard anything to the contrary, we would picket the pit on Monday morning and everything else would follow from that.

A social evening had long been arranged for the Saturday, with our friends from the Pendle area invited as a thank-you for all their efforts. Little did we realise when the date was agreed how momentous it would prove to be. Had we been aware of what was about to happen, I wonder if we would have planned in quite the same way.

The Pendle coach arrived at the strike centre around 3pm and it was wonderful to see the way the visitors were quickly absorbed and distributed among our own people; it was as if they had all known each other all their lives and the feeling of belonging was never stronger. With the strong possibility of a return to work the following week, they did their best to sympathise with and console us; the friendship

Pendle supporters join the strikers on the final weekend of the dispute *(John Lowe)*

John Lowe and Anne Campbell present Pendle Support Group with silver salver to show appreciation
(John Lowe)

and brotherhood with us they had displayed throughout the long months of strife was there to be seen on that evening, right when we were on the threshold of so much uncertainty in our lives. Their presence gave us an opportunity, for a few short hours, to delay facing the inevitable.

Later that day, we assembled in the local community centre. We were joined by a contingent from the London support group and also by a sizeable party from Wellingborough; needless to say, the evening was an overwhelming success with a great deal of emotion unashamedly on display. What was taking place on that night – although we had not given thought to it at that point – was the final farewell to a lot of wonderful people by a group which had, in effect, fought and lost a war. Many tears were openly shed on both sides; we sang, we danced and then we sang some more. We had fought as hard as we could, we had sacrificed so much; yet we still had our pride. We were entitled to shout it from the rooftops; if spirit alone won battles, the lads and their families would be invincible.

Sunday 3 March

This report is the hardest I've ever had to try and write. I feel so full of emotion – anger, frustration, shame, bewilderment. I'm finding great difficulty in putting my thoughts together. Perhaps it would have been better to leave it for a couple of days; I'm not sure.

Mid-afternoon the news came through that the conference had decided narrowly, 98 to 91, that the strike was at an end. Although expected, it came as a body blow, well below the belt. My wife cried tears for me that I couldn't cry for myself; they'll probably come later. I feel so proud of her for the support she's given in spite of all the difficulties and heartaches she's suffered. When the history of this dispute is written, the Elsie Lowes of this world will surely stand out above everything: Thatcher pales into insignificance and will never bear mention in the same breath. Hopefully we can get a good turnout for the final afternoon picket. I'd like us to show that we're still here and as defiant as ever; no one can take away our pride. Jim Dowen and myself will meet the colliery manager tomorrow to sort out the arrangements for our return: shift rotas, self-rescue tests, protective clothing reissue and, I suppose, whatever warnings he's been instructed to give. There's little we can do to help ourselves – we're in his hands. What we won't do is bloody well crawl! We have decided to hold what we hope will be the inaugural meeting of our '84 club;[1] much discussion centred around membership qualification and it was decided to draw a line through the Christmas break – lads who stayed out until then would be eligible. This

The emblem of the Black and Gold Social Club, which met for many years after the strike *(John Lowe)*

recommendation would be put to the first meeting. As for the £1,000 electricity bill from the welfare – the ladies demanded the right to decide what to do and a subsequent vote was unanimous to ignore it. Good for them!

Monday 4 March

We finish as we started – on the picket line. The police were there as usual to protect the scabs from 'intimidation'. On breakfast TV McLachlan was telling all and sundry for the umpteenth time how violent we'd been and what a good job he's been doing. How someone like him can be allowed to wield the authority he has is beyond anything that I can understand.

Picket managers' meeting at Ollerton at 10am: Henry Richardson gave a report on yesterday's day of shame at the Sheffield conference and confirmed what we had suspected – that it was the South Wales Area who had moved for the return to work. With so much we need to know in order to answer the questions our own lads will inevitably be asking on our arrival back at our own pits, the meeting was then broken up as Henry was due to address the Ollerton Branch meeting at 11am. I feel insulted – the delegates from the Notts strikers' representatives should have been his priority. Apart from drawing the picketing money it was wasted effort.

We arrived back in Clipstone at twelve noon to an amazing sight: the place was solid with police and the biggest picket we've had in a long time. The icing on the cake was the ladies – they had turned out in force along with the lads and the scabs were really getting it. Afterwards I felt exhilarated and for the rest of the afternoon was on a real high: we'd come in with a bang and we'd really gone out with one.

Clipstone ladies turn out for final day of picketing *(John Lowe)*

Section of picket outside pit-head baths and medical centre *(John Lowe)*

> Talks with the colliery manager were not completed until 1pm: he was prepared to talk frankly with us and all our questions were answered – to our advantage, we thought. Before leaving him we were even able to arrange for one of our lads to work day shift regular, if only for a month. Unlike the attitudes of some of the management in Notts, he was quite happy to give us the rota sheets to pass on to the lads and explain what was to happen the next day. At most pits in the county, this would be unthinkable and yes, we did recognise our good fortune in having a manager like John Daniels. We'd had a dialogue with him from the word go whereas at many pits those returning to work were being properly screwed; our return was made as smooth as possible by perhaps the only member of NCB management who had a principle in his body. Our fifty strikers were spread over three shifts at the pit; on his instructions, we were, where possible, placed in jobs with our own kind.
>
> We were, however, told that those who had been sacked by the NCB would remain sacked – a real body blow.

Monday 4 March (continued)

I am now coming to the end of these reports; for almost a year now I have tried to give a daily account of life at the Clipstone picket line. Unavoidably, it has included many other aspects of the dispute, which may seem repetitive to the reader. It has been the most wearing period of my life, and I wouldn't like to think so many good people will be put through such hardship and deprivation ever again; having said that, I wouldn't have missed the experience. In conclusion I would like to put on record for all time my appreciation for the loyalty of our Clipstone families to their union and to their colleagues both locally and nationally. My pride in being associated with such people will live with me forever – the great strike of 1984/85 will never be forgotten.

NATIONAL UNION OF MINEWORKERS/NOTTINGHAM AREA.

CLIPSTONE STRIKING MINERS AND LADIES SUPPORT GROUP.

Dear Friends,

Although we at Clipstone have returned to work, we assure
you that even though our hearts are heavy, our spirit is
not broken. Our sadness is mainly for our colleagues who
are not returning with us throughout the coalfields.

At many pits the Board are really turning the screws. In
Notts. even SCAB Branch Officials are joining with Management to try to break the lads who have gone back. This
they'll never do.

At Clipstone our experience has not been so bad as at some
local pits. Our total strength when we returned was 51.
We are committed, however, to continue the fight which is
now on two fronts.

Perhaps you won't have heard, as the media only tell what
they want you to know, but now the Notts. Area are threatening to expel we who have fought. So much for Mr. Lynk's
idea of democracy. Resisting him and his kind is the fight
which has to continue. We can assure you that we will continue to fight for jobs and communities, no matter where
the fight may be.

Everyone at the Clipstone Centre thanks you all for the
continued support you have so unstintingly given over these
long months. If people generally, and Certain National
Leaders in particular, had responded as yourselves, instead
of burying their heads, a different result would have been
achieved.

The friendships we have made must not be allowed to die.

Once again, thank you for your financial, physical and moral
support.

Yours still in struggle,

JOHN LOWE.
Chairman, Clipstone Strike Committee.

John Lowe defiant as he officially informs supporters of return to work *(John Lowe)*

Tuesday 5 March

I've tried to think through today of what the future holds. I feel anger at the outcome. We were let down by Areas who lost their nerve when faced with the experiences that we lived with throughout. I feel frustration at our inability to do anything about the situation. Shame I feel for much of the trade union movement, the Labour movement, our own class and particularly the scabby sort that I now have to live and work amongst. That our own people could sell out to an administration like Thatcher's should be unthinkable – well it's happened! Bewilderment; I still cannot put my thoughts into any reasonable sort of order. If I sit for long, my thoughts inevitably turn to the sell-out without being able to arrive at an explanation. The result of all these emotions is the worst feeling of helplessness I hope I'll ever have. Today has seemed like a nightmare ... first shift back – how do you work alongside people you despise? They, in turn, are giving us the cold shoulder. Truthfully, some are being civil and I suspect more would like to be, but many more are openly but quietly hostile. The feeling is mutual – but how long can we go on like this? Feeling really sick and ill tonight. Events these last three days have been like a funeral: one with Notts placed in the coffin alongside that corpse named 'hope'.

Wednesday 6 March

Day two of our return; without doubt there are many who will resent us for a long time – this much they make quite plain. While ever we are amongst them, their consciences cannot be at peace. Of course, there are those who are so blinded by ignorance that they have no conscience, but many do know the score and resent being made to feel uncomfortable. Feeling a little more composed now: I think cold anger, giving way perhaps to bitterness, will replace the heartache and sadness. I'm deliberately avoiding watching TV or reading newspapers for the present – this isn't trying to hide from reality, more an effort to regain my balance.

> On day two, N Pringle and I were virtually ignored, but if that was the worst they could manage then we had nothing to worry about. The morality was with us. We knew we had to be careful of our actions as any complaint from their side would be enough to warrant the sack for a striker. This was already happening at some pits.
>
> On reflection, I could see that this situation was happening in reverse in other Areas – and if given the choice, I would rather have been in our position in Notts than that of those in Yorkshire who had been outed as scabs. Not unnaturally, I hoped at that point that they were being given hell.

Friday 8 March

End of our first week back: the hurt will lessen, but I cannot see the bitterness going away for a long time. No one talks to us if they don't have to; in fairness, this is two-way traffic. The management are going a way to easing a tense situation by putting our lads to work together where possible, but there is a feeling amongst us that the trouble could start in two-to-three weeks – then they will be used to being back and the scabs will be arguing the

TUES. 5-3-85.

AND. AFTER.

I've tried to think through today of what the future now holds. Unfortunately my present state of mind will not allow deep thinking of any kind. The only conclusion I can reach at present is that I should continue to try to record what has become has become a very traumatic time for everyone returning. Without question this also includes their families.

I feel anger at the outcome. We were let down by Areas who lost their nerve when faced with the experience we had lived with throughout. Instead of fighting back within their Areas and taking their lads with them, too many 'bottled out'.

I feel frustration at our inability to do anything about the situation. We have had to stand and watch these same Areas decide to leave Notts out on a limb that could be broken at any time.

Shame I feel for much of the Trade Union and Labour movement, our class and particularly the SCABBY sort I now have to live and work amongst. That our own people could 'sell out' to an administration like Thatchers should be unthinkable. It's happened!

Bewilderment. At present I cannot put my thoughts into any reasonable sort of order. If I sit for long trying to think my thoughts

John Lowe's diary draws to an end *(John Lowe)*

rights and wrongs of what has happened. The danger then is that our lads will retaliate. Overtime is being worked extensively – it's frustrating that we can do sod all about it. Coal has been delivered today to a number of our lads – once again, the manager has played well by us.

I have to admit that my own attitude was most certainly aggressive and only N's common-sense approach made the atmosphere at times bearable. His was the more sensible way, considering we still had to work at the recruit back into the new Notts Area. His oft-repeated comments to me were: 'Lowey, y'se like oor next door neighbours' cat. Just when I've thrown doon the corn and got the birds feed'n', y'se jump doon and freet'n the buggers away.'

The women's group decided to make a payment of £12 to all the lads at the end of the first week back, a real boost. We also received a delivery of coal from the pit which was in direct contrast to the position at some of the others. Mansfield Colliery's manager, for example, had told the lads there that rest days could not be taken till they had been back at work for a full month – and that they could not expect a coal delivery for some time. Also strikers at some pits were forced to see their manager individually before they could return to work, which meant there was no full return on the Tuesday of this eventful week. In many cases the local branch officials were as involved as management in the persecution of returning strikers, who had the threat of dismissal always hanging over them.

The return to work nationally had signalled a display of the defiant spirit for which the miners have long been noted: the workforce at many collieries were seen on TV marching behind brassbands, with their women and children lining the streets of their villages in a show of solidarity. The message to Thatcher and her kind was plain: down, but not out. We in Notts, on the other hand, had to return without the fanfares and publicity; there were no bands to lead our lads through the villages and into the pit yards; there were no cameras to show our defiance in the face of defeat; people did not line the streets of our pit villages. This was Nottinghamshire: we were the minority and surrounded by hostility. The spirit of the lads on their return was nothing short of heroic. Not for over half a century had we seen a situation like this in the mining industry – and that had been the era of the Spencer union in Nottinghamshire. Nothing changes much, it seemed.

Conclusions

Having never been politically aware or active in the whole of my life, with only an elementary education, my qualifications for producing anything of literary value leave a lot to be desired; if, therefore, these diaries contain anything of interest, I can only assume it is because of the uncertainty day by day of the lives of a group of people involved with a desperate cause.

As I look back now many years later, bearing in mind how the dispute ended, the effect on the industry will not be much different to what it would have been had we not stood and fought. We now await the inevitable: the closure of all 'uneconomic capacity' and the privatisation of the 'profitable' sections of the industry are, we believe, just around the corner. Sadly, without the backing of our brothers in the trade union movement, the fight against such forces as those recently ranged against us is well-nigh impossible. All we can do is to try and fight back on a local basis – our chances at that level are almost non-existent.

Had we won the dispute, a different situation would have resulted: collieries and communities would have been saved; we would have been in a position to demand an energy strategy for the future, based on an expanding coal industry with imports kept in check; and a re-examination of the nuclear power programme would have shown the cost and potential for catastrophe involved in placing so much reliance on what has already been scrapped by the Americans as too dangerous. Our self-sufficiency should be prioritised above the obscene capitalist profit incentive which benefits a small number of the privileged in society. Had we won, a subsequent inquiry would have shown the collusion and intrigue that was practised against us: collusion between senior Board members and 'working miners' to tie up the National Union with so much legal action as to render it almost powerless; illegal police actions that enabled them to exceed their authority with impunity; the court practices which backed this and which have never before been experienced on such a scale in this country. The involvement of the 'special branch' was for me the most disturbing aspect: men arrested both on picket lines and away from them were subjected to a style of questioning not typically adopted in an industrial dispute, to say the least. The scale and intensity of the operation, when viewed from the inside, was frightening. Some mining communities will die, while many more will be adversely affected. In the present situation of unemployment, their chances for the future look grim – all this because the Board and the Government have embarked on a programme that takes no account of common sense or humanity.

The sort of recognition that we need for this industry and for many others will never be achieved under the present political system – even Labour administrations pay only lip service to what I now recognise as socialism. Too many vested interests across the whole political spectrum will ensure the continuation of the status quo. I've seen enough in twelve months to know that until the political mould is broken, the working class of this country can never move forward decisively.

I know that I will never be the same sort of person again. My faith in the impartiality of the police and justice under the law is destroyed forever; a whole set of values that my wife and I have lived our lives by has been smashed. Somehow and from somewhere we have to replace them with something worthwhile; this, I'm afraid, will be easier said than done.

My wife is still as wholeheartedly behind my stand as she was in the beginning. She has suffered heartache I would never voluntarily inflict upon her; the family problems associated with the dispute took her to the verge of a nervous breakdown. In spite of it all, I feel she has emerged a stronger personality, and has made many friends that under normal circumstances she would never have known.

> As for the lads and their wives, let me say I have never seen such genuine emotion and grief in my life as when the result of the special delegate conference was announced. The bond that was established between us will, we are determined, never be lost; the spirit of our people was far from broken; and the fight to maintain the continued existence of the National Union within Notts continues on.
>
> John Lowe, 1991

Notes
1. Black and Gold Social Club

AFTERWORD

The British mining industry was decimated by the Thatcher Government and is limited to a few deep and opencast mines today. Many of the communities situated around the pits have seen a rise in crime and drug use alongside unemployment.

British Coal closed Clipstone Colliery soon after John Lowe's reflection was written, in 1993. It was reopened privately the year after (April 1994) by RJB Mining, then closed for good in April 2003.

The headstocks which tower over the entrance from the Ollerton side of the village are the tallest in Europe and believed to be the third-tallest in the world. In 2005 the process of clearing the surrounding area of buildings was begun; now only the Grade II-listed winding gear remains upon sparse, levelled grassland – two ghostly monuments to the industry which gave birth to the village.

Clipstone headstocks and colliery buildings when pit was fully functional *(Andrew Symcox)*

John Lowe, centre, surrounded by strikers and supporters in Pendle at the time of the Silentnight Beds strike in the region *(John Lowe)*

The future of these remains in the balance, with many loath to see them go: an oft-repeated tale remarks upon their comforting sight when village folk return from their holidays. However, many people in Clipstone are keen to move on, with the estimated cost of maintenance of these dilapidated structures £70,000 a year.

My grandfather John Lowe kept a short diary during the miners' strikes of the 1970s, commented upon mining issues though verse – written in Midlands dialect – from that decade to the 1990s, authored a novella (*Benjie: A Socialist Dog*) from the point of view of a strike supporter's pet and wrote extensively about growing up in the 1930s and 1940s.

He died in 2005, leaving Elsie a widow, and is sorely missed by all his family.

For more information visit www.pen-and-sword.co.uk, including:

- Video of a walk around the cleared Clipstone Colliery site
- Video of an interview with Labour MP Dennis Skinner on the strike and John Lowe
- History of Clipstone pit village
- The arguments for and against keeping the headstocks
- Selected verse by John Lowe

Jonathan Symcox, 2011

LOYAL TO THE LAST

Davie Anderson
Bob Billings
John Bould
Andy Broadfoot
Doug Broadfoot
Gus Broadfoot
Glen Brownley
Roy Brownley
Hamish Campbell
Dan Carmody
Frank Childs
Sid Clayton
Dave Cook
Alan Cornell
Baz Cornell
John Cornell
Phil Crowder

Keith Davis
Jim Dowen
Neil Duncan
Martin Edwards
Andy Fisher
Mick Gibson
Jim Hall
Harry Harpham
Pete Harrison
Clayton Hood
Tommy Hood
Brent Howkins
Dave Huzij
Pat Hynes
Alan Jefferies
Benny Jefferies
Barry Jevons

Morris Langthorne
Dave Lankham
John Lowe
Eddie McSherry
Ray Neale
Andy Parkin
Derek Potter
Norman Pringle
Steve Radford
Morris Ripley
Johnny Sheffield
Alan Snaith
John Stone
Jim Strachan
Jack Taylor
Kev Thorpe
Jackie Waugh

INDEX

Germany 134
Gibson, M 91
Gillies, A 97
GLC/ County Hall (London) 49, 52–4, 56, 74
Gloucestershire police 47
GMBATU 54
Goose Fair Ground (Nottingham) 75
Government – see Conservative Party
Greatrex, Neil 91
Green, Joe 64–5
Grimsby 65, 151
Guardian, The 95

Hackett, Ernest 158–9
Hackett, Ida 6, 29, 48, 87, 158–9
Hackney Trades Council 49
Haldane Society 105
Hammand, Eric 167
Hampshire police 133, 152, 154
Harpham, H 28, 32, 37, 53, 60, 64, 75, 93, 95, 97
Hartley, R 47, 61, 97
Heathfield, Peter 151
Hemsley, Alf 27, 97
Herbert, B 50, 72, 84–5, 117
High Markham – see Trent Valley power stations
Holness, Jane 90
Hood, C 73, 120
Hood, Jim 50, 133, 144, 151
Hood, M 46, 52, 56, 58, 65, 74, 100–1
Hood, T 56
Hopkins & Sons (solicitors) 105
Houses of Parliament 54, 56–7, 89
Howarth, Mal 159
Howkins, B 149
Hucknall Colliery 54, 97, 103
Humber Bridge 83
Huzij, D 128

IBA 85, 86–7
'IL' 53, 66, 122, 126
ILP (Independent Labour Party) 89, 93
Ireland, Republic of 120

Ireland Colliery 125
Italy 134, 140
ITV 118, 142

'J' 132
'JB' (lawyer) 61
'JB' (retired NCB worker) 161
Jenkins, David, Bishop of Durham 107, 111
Jones, David Gareth 65, 108, 164
Jordon, Bill 167
Jubilee Gardens (London) 55

Kaufman, Gerald MP 122
Kent 74–5, 88–9, 143
King George Dock (Hull) 134
King's Cross (London) 55
Kinnock, Neil MP 126, 148, 167
Kiveton Park Colliery 103, 154–6, 160

'L' (Clipstone striker) 29
'L' (Sherwood scab) 120
Labour Party/movement – general 7, 15, 40, 66, 75, 80–1, 99, 102, 104–5, 107, 109, 122, 126, 128, 136, 145, 148, 157, 167, 174–5, 177
Laird, Gavin 167
Lancashire 52, 90
Lankham, D 73
Law Society 105, 119
Lawson, Nigel MP 159
Leicester 136
Leicestershire 137
Libya 118–19
Lido, Clipstone 29, 35, 39, 42
Linby Colliery 102
Lincoln prison 37, 70–2, 77, 107, 112
Liverpool 65
London 49–50, 52, 54–8, 65, 74, 77, 79, 88–9, 100–1, 133–4, 136, 141, 154, 160–1, 163–4, 169
London, Jack 24
London Metropolitan police – see Metropolitan police
London Zoo 89